he same authors

E ACOL SYSTEM TODAY
E BRIDGE PLAYER'S DICTIONARY
E PLAY OF THE CARDS

Bridge for
Tournament Pla

By

T
T
T

Bridge for Tournament Players

TERENCE REESE
and
ALBERT DORMER

ROBERT HALE & COMPANY
London

SBN 7091 0003 5

Robert Hale & Company
63 Old Brompton Road
London SW7

Printed in Great Britain by
Northumberland Press Limited
Gateshead, and bound by
James Burn & Co. Ltd., Esher

FOREWORD

This book has two main purposes: to describe the different sort of thinking that is needed in duplicate as compared with other forms of bridge; and to furnish the reader with the best bidding equipment.

In pursuing this second aim, we have struck a balance between new ideas and ideas that are firmly established. The fact is that, if one stands back and takes an unprejudiced look at current bidding theory, one finds many areas, especially in the competitive field, where improvement is possible. Very often, too, the improved method is no more complicated than the old method.

For several of our brighter notions we are indebted to Jeremy Flint, who returned from a season in North America with many fresh thoughts.

TERENCE REESE

ALBERT DORMER

CONTENTS

Part One
The Pairs Game

1 THE NEW OBJECTIVE   13

    Part-score bidding   15
    The game zone   17
    Slam bidding   19

2 COMPETITIVE AUCTIONS—THE RAZOR'S EDGE   22

    The disputed zone   22
    The sacrifice zone   25
    Doubles of freely bid contracts   27
    Summary of doubles   28
    Playing in a qualifying round   29

3 HOW TO PLAY POPULAR CONTRACTS   30

    'Unsafety' plays   31
    Estimating the popularity of your contract   33
    How the lead may affect your plan   34
    When to go down gracefully   37

4 LONG SHOTS AND SACRIFICES   40

    When there has been competitive bidding   42
    When you are doubled in a freely bid contract   45
    How to play sacrifice contracts   47
    Playing to the score   49

5 MATCH-POINT DEFENCE 51

    The opening lead 54
    Match-point tactics in the middle game 56

Part Two

Tournament Acol

6 TUNING UP THE SYSTEM 61

    Lighter but safer 61
    Responding on weak hands 62
    Second-round bids—forcing or not forcing? 63
    Nailing down the force in a new suit 64
    Introducing the Economical Jump 65
    What kind of no-trump? 68
    Opening 2NT 69
    Two bids 69
    Summary of the new proposals 72

7 COMPETITIVE MOVES IN DEFENCE 73

    The trap pass demoted 73
    New role for the cue-bid 74
    Making their suit your own 80
    Competitive manoeuvres by both sides after a
        1NT opening 82
    Doubling the response to 1NT 83
    Sequences following a 1NT opening and a
        conventional overcall 84
    Review of competitive moves 85
    After a 1NT opening 85

8 COMPETITIVE DOUBLES 87

    The responsive double 87
    Competitive doubles by the opening side 88
    Competitive doubles by the defending side 92
    Summary of the competitive double 95

Part Three

Conventions

9 REVITALISING THE OLD   99

Conventions after 1NT   99
Summary of responses to 1NT   103
Conventions after 2NT   103
Summary of sequences after 2NT   106
Conventions after 3NT   107
The Swiss Convention   107
Swiss for the minor suits   109
Other established conventions   110
Summary of changes in established conventions   112

10 BRINGING IN THE NEW   113

The new Roman   113
Trump asking bids   114
The Comic no-trump   115
Weak cue-bids   117
Modified Drury   119
Mainly about Aspro   124
Developments after an Aspro overcall   126
Summary of conventions   129
Shedding the load   130

11 VISIONS OF THE FUTURE   132

The relay principle   132
The transfer principle   133
The Interrogator   134
Light openings   135
Negative doubles   136
Advances in play   136
The Little Major   137

Part Four

Team-work

12 PLOTTING THE DEFENCE 151

Special leads 151
Signals and echoes 153
Signals at suit contracts 155
Signals at no-trumps 160
Three further messages 162
Summary of leads and signals 167

13 MATCH PLAY 168

The odds in an uncontested auction 168
The odds in a contested auction 169
The personal factor in match play 170
Preparing for a match 171
Rhythm in bidding and play 171
Morale 173

PART ONE

The Pairs Game

1

THE NEW OBJECTIVE

On, perhaps, seven hands out of ten the technique of bidding and play at duplicate is the same as at rubber bridge. But however well you play those seven, you won't pile up the master points until you adjust your methods on the other three. The first leap forward is the realisation that your real opponents are not the pair you are playing against, but the pairs sitting your way at the other tables.

<pre>
                       ♠ Q 10 6
                       ♡ K Q 5
                       ◇ 8 6 4 3 2
                       ♣ A 6
       ♠ A 7 3 2   ♠ 5 4
       ♡ 9   ♡ 10 8 6 3 2
       ◇ A 9 5   ◇ 10 7
       ♣ Q J 10 4 2   ♣ 9 8 7 5
                       ♠ K J 9 8
                       ♡ A J 7 4
   ♣ Q led   ◇ K Q J
                       ♣ K 3
</pre>

South is in 3NT and a club is led. At rubber bridge or team play there is no problem: drive out the Ace of spades and run for home when a club is returned. At duplicate (by which we mean always pairs play) it is not so simple, for the new objective is to beat as many other North-South pairs as possible, by however small a margin. If you settle for a safe nine tricks it is all too likely that the complete score-sheet will look something like this, yours being the final pathetic entry:

Pair No.			Contract	N-S Score	Match-points	
N-S		E-W			N-S	E-W
1	vs.	1	3NT by S	+430	6	6
2	vs.	3	3NT by N	+430	6	6
3	vs.	5	4H by S	+420	2	10
4	vs.	7	4Cx by W	+500	12	0
5	vs.	2	3NT by N	+430	6	6
6	vs.	4	4S by S	+450	10	2
7	vs.	6	3NT by S	+400	0	12

At duplicate you get two match-points for each pair sitting your way whose score you beat, plus one point for each pair you tie with. In this instance +400 earns no match-points. You receive, as the saying goes, a cold bottom.

All the other players who played in 3NT scored an over-trick—presumably because they attacked diamonds instead of spades. Had diamonds been 4-1 they would have lost the contract. Nevertheless, the risk was worth taking. The point is that they set themselves the correct objective—to beat other pairs playing the same way. Tackling diamonds instead of spades was the best means to that objective, for a 3-2 break is better than an even chance.

When playing this hand in 3NT you must not think only of other pairs in the same contract. It is reasonable to suppose that one or two will be in a major-suit game. If they score 450 you cannot hope to beat them, but if 420 is the limit in spades or hearts, again you need the overtrick in no-trumps.

Recognising the new objective is just as important in bidding as in play. With both sides vulnerable the bidding goes:

South	West	North	East
1♠	2◇	2♠	3◇
3♠	4◇	Pass	Pass
?			

South holds: ♠AK943 ♡KJ3 ◇82 ♣K105

South is clearly not worth Four Spades, so the choice is

whether to double or pass. The mathematics of rubber bridge do not favour a double when a one-trick penalty is all you can expect, but at the pairs game South must apply a different standard and consider what is likely to happen at the other tables.

Some pairs, at least, will be allowed to play in Two or Three Spades, making. The only way to beat them is by doubling Four Diamonds, converting a possible penalty of 100 points to 200—a magic number on part-score deals. If it turns out that West can make Four Diamonds the double is unlikely to cost many match-points, for minus 130 would have been a bad score anyway. By doubling you reduce your score from, perhaps, 2 to 0 if they make it; but if you get them one down you may improve from 5 to 12.

Bidding at duplicate is not much different from rubber bridge in the early rounds. The change is felt as you approach the final target. The technique varies according to the level of the contract—part-score, game, or slam—so we consider each of these separately.

PART-SCORE BIDDING

In the part-score zone the difference between duplicate tactics and normal bidding is slight. Of course, eight tricks at no-trumps beats eight and even nine in diamonds, but the no-trump contract tends to be more precarious. Also, you will not find such exact comparison as arises at the game level, when pairs may be in the same contract at almost every table. On a part-score deal there will be much more variation. In general, the aim is to play in the safest, not the most productive, part score. If there is no game on, + 110 will give you an average or better score, so do not run away from a safe Two Clubs to attempt a speculative 2NT. In the examples that follow there is mostly no difference between rubber bridge and duplicate tactics.

(1)	*South*	*North*
	1 ♣	1 NT
	?	

South holds: ♠ K J 5   ♡ Q 2   ◇ K J   ♣ K J 9 7 4 3

Bid Two Clubs. Lacking Aces, you may not have time to establish all your tricks at no-trumps.

(2)	South	North
	1 ♡	1 ♠
	?	

South holds: ♠ K 4   ♡ A K 10 7 2   ◇ A 9 6 3   ♣ J 3

Bid Two Diamonds. A rebid of hearts would not reflect the character of this medium-strength hand. Two Diamonds is the normal exploratory bid and the fact that it counts less than Two Hearts is unimportant.

(3)	South	West	North	East
	—	—	1 ♣	1 ♡
	?			

South holds: ♠ Q 8 7 2   ♡ J 4   ◇ A 8 2   ♣ 10 8 5 3

Bid Two Clubs, not One Spade. On a hand that is worth only one forward move, follow the sound principle of showing support for partner's suit.

(4)	South	North
	—	1 ♡
	?	

South holds: ♠ Q 10 4   ♡ J 4   ◇ K 9 4 3   ♣ A 7 5 2

Bid 1NT. This is one of the few situations in the part-score area where it can be correct to bid differently at duplicate. At rubber bridge or team play you would respond Two Clubs because 1NT is a slight underbid and might cause you to miss game. But at duplicate 1NT is a *good* contract and in the long run it will pay to play there, scoring overtricks, rather than in a shaky game.

We said earlier that duplicate considerations seldom intrude in the first round of bidding. An exception is the borderline third- or fourth-hand opening. At duplicate the search for a plus score is so intense that players tend to open moderate balanced hands which at rubber bridge would be thrown in. Such openings are safest when they contain some support for any suit responder may bid, so that the opener will not have to bid again.

(1) ♠K7653   ♡5   ◇AJ84   ♣Q72

(2) ♠KQ83   ♡Q4   ◇A104   ♣10973

Hand (1) is a doubtful One Spade opening in third or fourth position because if partner responds Two Hearts or 2NT a minus score is likely.

On hand (2) it is tolerably safe at any score to open One Spade, with the intention of passing the response. Note that at rubber bridge it would be the other way round. You might open One Spade on the first hand, because game is not impossible. But to open the second hand with the object of snatching a part score would not be worth the risk of being carried too high.

When responding to a third- or fourth-hand opening it is wise to allow some leeway. Prefer a maximum 1NT response to a bid in a moderate suit at the Two level; prefer a One-over-One response to a rubber-bridge 2NT; above all, avoid the monstrosity of 3NT.

In a later chapter we describe the Drury Convention, which is specially designed to allow for sub-standard openings in third and fourth hand.

THE GAME ZONE

In the game zone the special objectives of duplicate bidding appear much more clearly. For a start, the odds about bidding a game are different. At rubber bridge and team play it pays to bid a game that is slightly against the odds. In pairs it doesn't. There is no point in going for game unless you will have a 50% chance of beating the pairs who don't bid it. You will in fact score quite well if you bid only games that are even money or better. Therefore, if at rubber bridge you would be uncertain whether to raise partner from Two Hearts to Three, from 1NT to 2NT, or from 2NT to 3NT, play for the plus score. Plus 140 or 120 can be worth a bomb.

When you hold game values, the problem may be where to play. It is well to recognise at the outset that you are seldom going to play in Five of a minor. In many situations a blind

bid of 3NT is better than a scientific investigation. You open
One Club and partner raises to Three Clubs. Your hand is:

(1) ♠102   ♡A4   ◇A1076   ♣AQ10 5 3

(2) ♠J9   ♡AJ8   ◇AK2   ♣AQ1043

On (1) the sensible action at rubber bridge would be to test
partner with Three Diamonds, expecting to finish either in
3NT or Five Clubs. In a pairs you must bid 3NT. You will
win no medals for scoring 600 in Five Clubs when others are
scoring 630 or 660 in 3NT with the help of a lucky lead or a
finesse. Of course, Five Clubs may be the only possible game
contract; but that is a narrow target and in practice you
should play with the field in 3NT.

On (2) there are slam possibilities and again the normal
move would be Three Diamonds, to be followed by a cue-bid
in hearts. However, so far as opener can judge at this stage,
the odds are against reaching a good slam. As you cannot afford
to end up in Five Clubs, settle for 3NT.

Here is another situation where it is advisable to back-
pedal so that you stay within range of 3NT:

South	North
—	1 ♡
1 ♠	2 ◇
?	

South holds: ♠AK5 3   ♡86   ◇KQ10 2   ♣108 3

At rubber bridge Four Diamonds is the right bid. In a pairs
it is better to bid only Three Diamonds. You might, as an
alternative, bid the fourth suit, Three Clubs, inviting partner
to bid 3NT if he holds the clubs; but this sequence would
conceal the main feature, your diamond support. The fourth
suit would be a better solution in a case like this:

South	North
—	1 ♠
2 ♣	2 ◇
?	

South holds: ♠A8   ♡A2   ◇J853   ♣KJ873

A bid of Two Hearts, asking partner to clarify his hand, is certainly more attractive than an underbid of Three Diamonds or a jump to Four.

Sometimes in the course of slam exploration you will arrive at Five Diamonds or Five Clubs and be sorry you have left 3NT behind. On such occasions you must bid the minor-suit slam if you think there is any chance of making it, for $+400$, if your assumption about 3NT is correct, will surely be a poor result.

A critical sector of bidding is the choice between game in a major and game in no-trumps. The extra scoring power of the first trick at no-trumps does not mean that a no-trump game is more to be preferred at duplicate than at other forms of scoring. In general, the reverse is true because more often than not a sound trump contract will produce an extra trick. So, when you judge that game will be easy whether you play in the major suit or no-trumps, prefer the major suit; but when game itself is borderline, incline towards the nine-trick contract. One good reason is that, in general, opponents are more likely to slip up against 3NT than against Four Hearts or Four Spades.

A frequent problem is whether to use the Stayman Convention after partner has opened 1NT. Many points are lost through mistaken tactics on this sort of hand:

♠QJ52   ♡82   ◇AQ8   ♣K952

When partner opens a strong no-trump, do you bid Two Clubs or do you raise straight to 3NT? There is a difference here between rubber bridge and duplicate. On general principles, if you hold more than enough points for game, no-trumps will be *safer* than a trump contract which may be upset by bad breaks or by a ruffing defence. At rubber bridge or team play, therefore, you would raise to 3NT. At duplicate you aim to be top of the class; you bid Two Clubs, because if partner holds four spades you may out-score the field.

SLAM BIDDING

A small slam should be at least an even-money chance at any kind of scoring, but the odds required for a grand slam vary.

At rubber bridge the slam should be at least 2-1 on. In a match between two equal teams it should be about 6-4 on. In a pairs you must take into account what is likely to happen at other tables. If everyone is going to be in at least Six—seldom a safe assumption—you want to be in any grand slam that is better than an even-money chance; but if some pairs will not be in a slam at all you stand to gain much less by bidding Seven and need very good odds. Chancing Seven when half the opposition has failed to progress beyond game is as superfluous as a lap of honour by a Grand National winner.

When it does seem that most of the field will be in a slam, the mathematical odds to justify Seven may be expressed as 'a finesse at worst'. One can quite often assess a hand in those terms. A grand slam with nine trumps, missing the Queen, is a sound proposition.

Another critical situation is where there is a choice between two slam contracts at the same level. In theory, the high-value contract should be preferred if it is perceptibly better than a 50% chance, even though the low-value contract may seem more secure. In practice, if you follow that principle you will be taking bad odds whenever part of the field fails to reach the slam. Psychology and a knowledge of other players' methods come into the reckoning. On the following hand South has to decide whether to bid Six Clubs or 6NT.

South	North
1 ♣	2 ♡
3 ♣	4 ♣
4 NT (B'wd)	5 ◇
?	

South holds: ♠ A Q   ♡ Q 7   ◇ K 3 2   ♣ A Q 9 6 3 2

With a strong opening opposite partner's jump shift, South, in an experienced field, should expect everyone to reach the obviously safe contract of Six Clubs. No one will bid Seven with an Ace missing, so the question is whether 6NT is likely to be better than an even chance. If North holds the King of hearts, the suit in which he forced, twelve tricks will be as easy in no-trumps as in clubs. On the simple ground that North is likely to hold that King, South should bid 6NT.

Here the opposite argument applies because the bidding is far from automatic:

South	North
—	1NT (15-17)
2♣	2♦
4♣	4♠

South holds: ♠Q4 ♡KJ94 ◇AQ7 ♣A1082

South's bid of Four Clubs has shown a four-card club suit plus the values for a quantitative bid of 4NT. (See page 102.) North's Four Spades agrees clubs and shows the Ace of Spades. As South, you now reckon that playing in clubs may be worth an extra trick, and that some pairs will lack the machinery to locate the 4-4 fit. So, be content to play in a good slam that many pairs will miss. You are playing duplicate, it is true, but don't forget to play bridge.

2

COMPETITIVE AUCTIONS—
THE RAZOR'S EDGE

We turn now to competitive bidding. Here duplicate players live on the razor's edge. Remarks like 'I was afraid of pushing them into game', 'It costs 500 if we sacrifice', 'I couldn't come in on eight points', are the soft soap of rubber-bridge post-mortems, but at duplicate they represent defeatism. As in a doubles final at Wimbledon, you have to be up at the net, fighting all the time.

In later chapters we suggest various new techniques in competitive bidding. For the present we are concerned with tactics rather than method. We study tactics, first in the disputed zone, where the strength of the two sides is evenly matched; secondly, in the sacrifice zone; and thirdly, in relation to doubles of freely bid contracts.

THE DISPUTED ZONE

Except in a high-powered game where the battle is keen and the standard high, rubber-bridge players do not take risks to compete in the part-score area. Up to a point they are right. It is depressing to lose 300 to save a part score; it is galling to get opponents one range higher and then be punished by an unintelligent partner who supports your venturesome call; and it is maddening to find that opponents were underbidding in the first place and can now either proceed to game or administer a punishing double. At duplicate, except against really weak players, one assumes that opponents who die early lack the values for game, and that your side is not far behind in high cards.

You must be very unwilling to let opponents make a comfortable part score on a hand where you are not obviously outgunned. With neither side vulnerable the bidding has gone:

South	West	North	East
—	—	—	1 ♠
Pass	2 ♠	Pass	Pass
?			

You hold as South:

(1) ♠A 8 2   ♡6   ◇K J 6 3   ♣Q 10 7 5 3

Reopen with an 'unusual' 2NT, inviting partner to bid a minor suit. If opponents go to Three Spades you may have sufficient defence.

(2) ♠9   ♡Q 10 4   ◇A 10 7 4 2   ♣K J 8 2

Reopen with a double. Some players would have doubled on the first round, but that goes a little far. Now your hand is limited, and it is reasonable to suppose that partner will have some values.

(3) ♠K 8 7 4   ♡A Q 3   ◇K Q 10 5   ♣10 6

Again, step in with a double. Partner will be short in spades, so may have a fit in a red suit or enough clubs to escape a double by the opponents. If he bids Three Clubs and opponents go to Three Spades, you can expect to beat them. If Three Clubs is doubled, you may consider an S.O.S. redouble.

Of course, any of these calls could turn out badly and would be unsound at rubber bridge except with a strong partner.

We look next at problems in the so-called 'balancing' position. With neither side vulnerable, the bidding has gone:

South	West	North	East
—	1 ◇	Pass	1 ♡
Pass	2 ◇	Pass	Pass
?			

You hold as South:

(1) ♠K 6 2   ♡K J 7 4   ◇8 6   ♣A 9 3 2

Reopen with a double. Any aggressive rubber-bridge player

would do the same here. You may be in the penalty market if partner has diamonds.

(2) ♠K 10 6 5 ♡A 8 6 5 ◇7 4 2 ♣K Q

Compete with Two Spades. The suit may seem weak, but it is most unlikely that left-hand opponent will be able to double. It is not unknown to contest even in a three-card suit when you feel, 'If we can get them one higher. . . .'

(3) ♠A 6 ♡K J 8 4 3 ◇7 3 ♣J 8 6 5

Compete with Two Hearts, the enemy suit, rather than let them play unchallenged in Two Diamonds.

Whether or not you favour the practice of marking the domestic linen His or Hers, you must decide whether a part-score hand is Yours or Theirs. If you feel that the opponents have the balance you must not hesitate to risk a loss of 100 by competing. 'Disciplined boldness' is the watchword.

South	West	North	East
—	1 ♡	Double	Redouble
2 ♣	Pass	Pass	2 ♡

Neither side is vulnerable and you hold as South:

♠Q 8 ♡9 2 ◇K 9 6 5 ♣J 9 5 4 3

If partner has a reasonable double you can probably make eight tricks in one of the minor suits and you may have a defence to Three Hearts. The best call now is 2NT. This cannot be genuine, so partner will realise that you have competitive prospects in clubs and diamonds. Vulnerable, this manoeuvre would be dubious, at any rate against strong opponents who would be poised to double in the hope of picking up 200.

It follows in the same way that when the deal belongs to your side you must not accept a penalty of 100. A typical match-point situation arises after this bidding:

South	West	North	East
—	—	1 ♡	1 ♠
1NT	2 ♠	3 ♡	Pass
Pass	3 ♣	Pass	Pass
?			

Still with neither side vulnerable, you hold as South:

♠ A 10 3   ♡ J 8 4   ◇ K 10 7 2   ♣ 7 6 4

First of all, how do you assess the chances? Partner did not double Three Spades, despite your free bid of 1NT, so you cannot expect this to be more than one down. As partner's bid of Three Hearts was competitive, Four Hearts must also be doubtful and may be doubled, for opponents know you were willing to pass the hand out in a part score.

You must nevertheless bid Four Hearts for this reason: to let opponents play in Three Spades undoubled can scarcely be good, and to double and take a penalty of 100 will not be good enough if other pairs are scoring 110 or 140 your way. So you hope either to make Four Hearts a bit luckily or possibly to drive opponents to Four Spades. It is true that by going to Four Hearts over Three Spades you may be exchanging plus 50 for minus 50 or minus 100, but on the match-point sheet those results will be close together.

If both sides were vulnerable this would be a difficult decision. Again, it would be wrong to let opponents play in Three Spades undoubled. You would just have to decide which was more likely—that you could pick up 200 by doubling, or that you could make Four Hearts or go one down undoubled.

Hands where the contest is at the game level or above may also belong to the disputed zone. When both sides are close to game and the problem is whether to double Four Spades, say, or bid on to Five Hearts, the rubber-bridge rule is well known: when in doubt, bid one more. In a team game, too, to lose 790 when you could have made a higher contract your way is disaster. In a pairs it is just one bad board, no more serious in its effect than any other bad board. If you judge that the odds are slightly against their making Four Spades and slightly against your making Five Hearts, you must double.

THE SACRIFICE ZONE

Just as the mathematics of sacrifice bidding are different from rubber bridge, so are the tactics. First of all, you must make light overcalls and take risks to get into the bidding when there is a chance of a profitable save. When you find a fit you must push on to the uttermost. Calculating players at rubber bridge do not fall over themselves to yield 500, or even 300, to save a game that is less than certain, nor do they draw fine distinctions according to the vulnerability. But in duplicate a sacrifice that costs 500 is a triumph if the opponents are vulnerable, a black disaster if they are not.

On the following deal North-South would probably not even enter the bidding at rubber bridge. At duplicate everyone has problems.

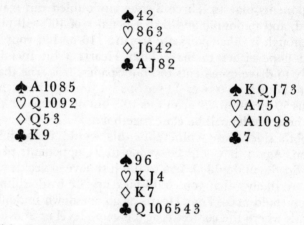

```
                    ♠ 4 2
                    ♡ 8 6 3
                    ◇ J 6 4 2
                    ♣ A J 8 2

   ♠ A 1 0 8 5                      ♠ K Q J 7 3
   ♡ Q 1 0 9 2                      ♡ A 7 5
   ◇ Q 5 3                          ◇ A 1 0 9 8
   ♣ K 9                            ♣ 7

                    ♠ 9 6
                    ♡ K J 4
                    ◇ K 7
                    ♣ Q 1 0 6 5 4 3
```

With East-West vulnerable, the bidding goes:

South	West	North	East
—	Pass	Pass	1 ♠
2 ♣	3 ♠	4 ♣	4 ♠
5 ♣	Double	All pass	

At rubber bridge South would not overcall with Two Clubs, for his partner has passed and the bid does not deprive the enemy of much bidding space. Playing duplicate, at this particular vulnerability, he takes the risk because it may lead to a sacrifice. South's bid of Five Clubs, inviting an almost certain 500, would also be wrong at rubber bridge.

As the bidding has actually gone, at duplicate, both West and East have defensive rather than eleven-trick hands, so it is clear that they should double on the final round. But suppose you strengthen the East hand a little, giving him:

♠ K Q 10 8 3 2   ♡ A 7 5   ◇ A 10 9 8   ♣ —

Now he should be unwilling to accept the penalty, for there must be a good chance of registering 650. In general, a vulnerable pair must go for the game, especially when notorious pushers have entered the bidding and found a fit. It is no use accepting 500 when at every other table the pairs playing your way have scored a comfortable 620 or 650. By going to Five Spades in the present example you challenge opponents to enter the 700 zone.

Finally, sacrifices against slam contracts are overdone by many players. If you save against a vulnerable slam and lose 900 you may acquire a virtuous glow, but few match-points. Too often, other pairs playing your way will have conceded 680 or perhaps 700, having been doubled at a lower range. It is better, in general, to take your chance on beating the slam.

Slam sacrifices in pairs are advisable only in two circumstances. One is when the weight of the enemy bidding suggests that the slam will be universal and by some competitive manoeuvre you have found a path to a sacrifice. The other time is when you have been competing normally up to the Four or Five level and may be able to sacrifice at a cost that will give you the advantage over the pairs who have yielded 680.

DOUBLES OF FREELY BID CONTRACTS

Borderline doubles of voluntarily bid games are less to be recommended than at rubber bridge. Take the familiar position where opponents bid with some hesitation to 3NT and you can tell that the cards do not lie well for them. An aggressive player at rubber bridge will double freely and often pick 300 or more out of the air. At duplicate, if you get them two down you will score well already, for some pairs will not be in game.

In the same way, you must not be in a hurry to double a borderline Four Hearts or Four Spades because you hold four trumps or place your partner with four trumps. Experienced declarers will conclude at once that the trumps are not breaking and may save a trick in the play. In general, it is wrong to double *venturesome* contracts, either at game or slam level. If you are right in considering them to be venturesome, you don't need to press.

On the other hand, it is right to double a confidently bid slam which, from possession of specific cards, you judge to be headed for the rocks. Suppose, for example, that the bidding has made it plain that the opponents are missing an Ace, and you happen to hold Q J x of trumps, or K x over the strong hand: a double will pay handsomely if the slam is bid generally, but it is a needless risk against a pair of overbidders.

What about doubles of 1NT? Weak and ultra-weak no-trump openings are so common, and the doubling, rescuing and competitive manoeuvres so diverse, that we make a special study of the subject in Chapter 7. For the present, our only observation is that if you think your opponents have chosen the wrong moment to open 1NT, you don't necessarily have to double. Suppose a vulnerable opponent opens a 12-14 no-trump as West and after two passes you survey:

♠ K 10 7 2   ♡ A J 6   ◇ Q 4   ♣ K J 7 3

There is a temptation to apply the axe. Resist it. East may be lurking and in that case your interference will cost you 300 or more. If North, your partner, has eight or nine points and you defeat 1NT by two tricks, plus 200 will surely be well above average. If you defeat it by only one trick, it is far from certain that other North-South pairs will have scored better on your cards.

Many players who have a generally good understanding of match-point tactics make poor doubles. You can be a good doubler if you ask yourself the simple question: Do I need to double?

SUMMARY OF DOUBLES

(1) *Competitive part-score hands.* If the hand belongs to your side and the opponents are pushing, you must take risks for a penalty of 200 or more. It is not a disgrace to double the enemy into game from time to time. Indeed, if this never happens you are not doubling often enough. But when the hand belongs to the other side and you are doing the pushing,

do not double the final contract. If you get them one down, that will probably be sufficient reward.

(2) *Competitive game hands.* If opponents are clearly defending, you must double, because now plus 100 instead of plus 50 will be a common result. Anyway, you have nothing to hope for if they make their contract, even undoubled. On really close hands, where eventually you decide not to go for game your way, it is unnecessary to double. If you have taken the right view you will score well enough.

(3) *Sacrifices.* When vulnerable, be willing to be pushed one range higher by non-vulnerable opponents, provided the odds are still in favour of making your game contract.

(4) *Freely-bid contracts.* Don't rush to double venturesome contracts. But when a popular contract seems to be in jeopardy, double even for a small gain.

PLAYING IN A QUALIFYING ROUND

The general tactics we have described in this chapter are tactics for winning. If you are playing in a qualifying round where, perhaps, a third of the field will go into the final, of course you will not need to play so sharp a game. Seek now to avoid calamities and to get a steady run of average scores. The occasional 'sweetener' will come along of its own accord.

3

HOW TO PLAY POPULAR
CONTRACTS

The special challenge of card play at duplicate is that the target, in terms of tricks, may be neither clear nor stationary. It may be necessary to aim higher than your contract—or lower. A declarer who fails to consider this may waste his efforts, like a marksman who aims at the wrong circle.

The first point to study when the dummy goes down is the quality of the contract. Is it good or bad? Obvious or rare? In this chapter we look at the obvious, or 'popular', contracts.

When everyone is likely to be in the same contract, simply to make it is not a primary objective. What counts is to make more tricks than the other players, whether enough for contract or not. Suppose you are in Four Spades; you have two losers in the plain suits and this is the trump situation:

North
10 7 6 3

South
A Q 8 5 2

At rubber bridge you would cash the Ace before leading up to the Queen. At duplicate, in a popular contract, you cannot afford that sort of safety play. Your aim is to make plays that will beat other plays more often than not. Cashing the Ace gains when West holds a singleton King, but the finesse is better when East holds a doubleton King—much more likely. The fact that the safety play helps to ensure the contract, and the finesse merely stands to gain an overtrick, does not alter the situation.

On the following hand it is not so easy to determine which play gives the best chance to beat the field. South is in Four Hearts and expects everyone else to be in the same spot.

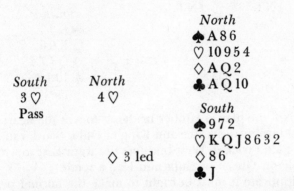

```
                              North
                              ♠ A 8 6
                              ♡ 10 9 5 4
                              ◇ A Q 2
                              ♣ A Q 10
   South      North
   3 ♡        4 ♡
   Pass                       South
                              ♠ 9 7 2
                              ♡ K Q J 8 6 3 2
              ◇ 3 led         ◇ 8 6
                              ♣ J
```

A rubber-bridge player would see a safe route to ten tricks. Win the opening lead with ◇ A, cash ♣ A and lead ♣ Q, discarding a loser if East does not cover. At duplicate South has to consider whether to play for an overtrick by finessing ◇ Q at trick 1. If the finesse holds, South plays clubs next and loses only one trick in the black suits. But if the diamond finesse loses and a spade comes back, he is in danger of losing his contract. Even so, it is the right play at duplicate.

'UNSAFETY' PLAYS

To refuse the diamond finesse on the hand above would be an 'unsafety' play in the sense that while slightly improving the chances of contract it reduces the expectation of tricks. The next hand is another example:

North
♠ 6 4 2
♡ A 2
♢ A K 9
♣ A K J 8 3

South   *North*
—   1 ♣
1NT   3NT
Pass

South
♠ K 9 3
♡ K 9 6
♢ Q J 7 4
♣ 10 4 2

♡ 8 led

In 3NT the play at rubber bridge is to win the heart open-ing and lay down the Ace and King of clubs. South can afford to lose a club trick to West but does not want East to win with a doubleton Queen of clubs and lead a spade.

At duplicate it must be right to make the normal percent-age play in clubs. Win the heart lead in dummy and cash ♣ A; run the diamonds and then lead ♣ 10, intending to finesse. This sequence of play loses when East holds ♣ Q x and may cost the contract if ♠ A is on the wrong side as well; but the club finesse gains on the more numerous occasions when West holds Q x x or Q 9 x x.

One can almost say that in a popular contract a safety play has virtue only when it is likely to gain rather than cost a trick. Compare these two familiar combinations:

(1)   *North*
      K Q 7 4 3

      South
      A 6 2

(2)   *North*
      A K Q 7 4

      South
      6 2

South is in 3NT and has no re-entry to dummy. Even if he needs exactly four tricks for his contract, he should not duck a round with the first combination. That would be an unsafety play, because the 3-2 break is appreciably more likely than 4-1. (Note, though, that there is still a correct way to play the com-bination: cash the Ace, then low to dummy so that you will be able to duck if West shows out.) With (2) the duck is not an unsafety play because in the long run the play to make four tricks will be more rewarding than the attempt to make five.

ESTIMATING THE POPULARITY OF YOUR CONTRACT

On many hands declarer cannot make a rational choice between two plays without considering what may happen at other tables. A knowledge of your competitors' methods may be worth points on a deal like this:

North
♠ 10 2
♡ K 3 2
◇ A J 10 5
♣ A 8 4 3

South	*North*
1NT	3NT
Pass	

South
♠ A J 9
♡ A 8 6
◇ 7 6 4
♣ Q J 10 7

♠ 4 led

You open a non-vulnerable weak no-trump and are raised to game. A spade is led and you capture East's King with the Ace. The club finesse works and after clearing the suit you lead a diamond, the Jack losing to the Queen. The 8 of spades comes back and the Jack holds. With the defenders poised to take three spade tricks, do you risk another diamond finesse or settle for nine tricks?

First, it is useful to know that the second finesse in diamonds is not an even chance but nearly 2 to 1 on. (This, putting it one way, is because East was initially more likely to hold one honour than two, and nothing has happened to change that.) Whether you should play for this superior chance depends on whether or not you expect other pairs to be in game. If not, then clearly you should be satisfied with 400. The deciding factor here is whether the 12-point no-trump is the fashion. If it is, then other pairs will bid the same way; if it isn't, then some pairs may not reach game.

This was rather a special case, because the bidding could

be related to the opening 1NT. We do not suggest that declarer need always give thought to the bidding habits of players at other tables; in some schools you might as well study a goose's entrails. One goes on general impressions—for example, if the hands are balanced and there are 25 points, most pairs will be in 3NT. If there is a 4-4 major, most pairs will play there.

When in doubt, the rule is simple: play for a plus score. This is especially true of hands where there is competitive bidding. How often, on a competitive deal, do you pick up the travelling score slip and see all the scores one way? Very seldom, so take a plus score and be on the side of the angels.

HOW THE LEAD MAY AFFECT YOUR PLAN

The opening lead is important in a sense that does not arise at rubber bridge. Suppose you get a favourable lead: then you must play to keep a step ahead of the field.

North
♠ K 6 4
♡ A J 5
◇ 10 3
♣ Q 10 8 7 2

South	*North*
1NT	3NT
Pass	

South
♠ A J 7
♡ K 7 4 2
◇ A 8 5
♣ K J 4

♠ 2 led

After scrabbling around for some uncomfortable moments, West leads a low spade and you head the 10 with the Jack. You knock out the Ace of clubs and win the diamond return. You have ten tricks on top and the question is whether you play for more by finessing ♡ J. At this point you should think back to the opening lead. Players don't usually rush to lead from Q x x x against 3NT, so probably a diamond will be led at some tables. As you were off to a lucky start, accept ten tricks, which may well give you a good score.

Here is another hand where you should determine not to lose the advantage of a favourable lead:

North
♠ A 7
♡ K 5 3 2
◇ Q 10 8 3 2
♣ 8 3

South	*North*
1 ♡	3 ♡
4 ♡	Pass

♣ 5 led

South
♠ 10 8 3
♡ A J 10 6
◇ K J
♣ A K 7 6

You open One Heart and finish in Four Hearts. West leads a club and you win with the Ace. Now you have a chance to get the diamonds going before spades are attacked. Opponents win the first diamond and play spades. You could win and play trumps in the normal way, finessing the Jack, but if it lost to the Queen you would end up with only ten tricks. Best is to cash ♡ A-K and then hope to discard your spade losers before an opponent can ruff. That offers the best chance to beat the declarers who opened One Club (as many will) and had to contend with a spade lead.

Do not conclude that when you get a favourable lead you should always play cautiously thereafter. Quite often, the way to stay a move ahead is to do what you think other declarers will do, no matter whether that involves bold play or safe play. Like the secret agents of spy fiction, you 'tail' your quarry from in front.

North
♠ A 8 2
♡ A J 8
◇ A 8 7
♣ J 7 5 4

South	*North*
1NT	3NT
Pass	

♡ 10 led

South
♠ J 5 4
♡ K 7 6
◇ K 9 2
♣ A K 9 2

South is in 3NT and West leads ♡ 10, covered by Jack,

Queen and King. It looks as though West has presented you with an extra heart trick by leading from 10 9 x. It would be a mistake now to take the safety play in clubs, cashing the Ace and leading low towards the Jack. Other pairs, needing four tricks from the suit, will lay down the Ace and King of clubs. To make sure of retaining your lead if the Queen is doubleton, you must do the same.

The next hand shows the other side of the coin: after an unwelcome lead you have to follow an unusual line to hoist yourself off the floor.

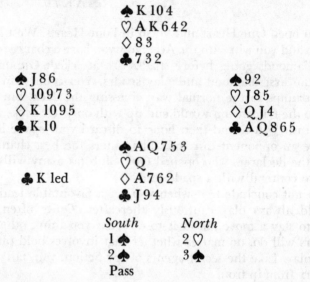

♠ K 10 4
♡ A K 6 4 2
♢ 8 3
♣ 7 3 2

♠ J 8 6   ♠ 9 2
♡ 10 9 7 3   ♡ J 8 5
♢ K 10 9 5   ♢ Q J 4
♣ K 10   ♣ A Q 8 6 5

♠ A Q 7 5 3
♡ Q
♣ K led   ♢ A 7 6 2
♣ J 9 4

South	North
1 ♠	2 ♡
2 ♠	3 ♠
Pass	

The part-score contract in spades looks normal, but West in hostile fashion strikes the lead of the King of clubs. The defenders take three club tricks and switch to a diamond.

The situation is not very favourable, for declarers who do not get a club lead are likely to make ten tricks by way of five spades, three hearts, Ace of diamonds and a diamond ruff. To enter the lists at a respectable level you must win with ♢ A, cash ♡ Q, and finesse ♠ 10 for an additional entry to dummy. If all goes well you get three diamond discards on the hearts and score an average with 170.

When assessing the opening lead, a point to bear in mind is that other pairs may play the same contract the other way up.

North
♠ K 7 5 3
♡ A Q J
♢ Q 10 4
♣ A 10 3

South	*North*
—	1NT
3♠	4♠
Pass	

South
♠ A J 8 6 2
♡ K 9 4 3
♢ 8 6 2
♣ Q

♢ 3 led

The defenders take three diamond tricks, East holding
A J x, and exit with a heart. If you were playing rubber bridge
you would probably play off Ace and King of trumps. Playing
duplicate, you must reflect that the contract will often be
played by North, for over 1NT many South players will bid
a conventional Two Clubs. East is unlikely to lead a diamond
from his hand, so if the trumps are 2-2 North will make eleven
tricks. You must hope the trumps are not breaking and must
seek to draw level by playing East for ♠ Q x x.

WHEN TO GO DOWN GRACEFULLY

As at poker, there is an art in losing the minimum. At
rubber bridge the declarer will take any chance for his contract, unless a heavy penalty is threatened. At duplicate, to
accept one (or more) down is one of the standard ways of winning match-points.

North
♠ A K 5 2
♡ K J
♢ Q 8
♣ A 10 8 5 3

South	*North*
—	1♣
1♢	1♠
1NT	2NT
3NT	Pass
Pass	

South
♠ 10 8 4
♡ A Q
♢ K 10 7 5 3
♣ J 9 4

♡ 2 led

The heart lead against 3NT makes an immediate dent in South's defences. At rubber bridge he would try to make four tricks in diamonds, as it would be worth while going down a couple of extra tricks in an attempt to make game. At duplicate you expect everyone to be in 3NT and may stage a small killing by attacking clubs, taking two finesses. By following the odds-on chance, even though it stands to win only eight tricks, you will be favourite to beat pairs who set their sights on game.

A very common situation arises on this hand:

North
♠ 8 5 3
♡ A 7 6 3
◇ K J 9
♣ 7 4 2

South	North
1 ♠	1NT
3 ♠	4 ♠
Pass	

♣ K led

South
♠ A K J 7 4 2
♡ 10 8
◇ A 6
♣ Q J 10

West cashes two top clubs, then switches to a low heart. You go up with the Ace and play off two high spades, East throwing a club on the second round. Now you must decide whether to risk two down by finessing ◇ J in an attempt to make the contract.

West has turned up with ♣ A K and ♠ Q, and his lead of a low heart suggests an honour in this suit. There is still room for him to hold the Queen of diamonds and at rubber bridge you would play for that possibility. At duplicate you are faced with the straight question: who is more likely to hold ◇ Q? The answer is East, so, playing in an obviously popular contract, you accept one down.

On some hands, especially those where there is a choice between 3NT and game in a major suit, you may judge that you are in a 'semi-popular' contract, the field being divided. Now it may be necessary to address your mind to the likely fate of players in the other group.

North
♠ Q 9 7
♡ 7 6 3 2
◇ A K 5
♣ 6 4 3

South	*North*
1 ♠	2 ♠
4 ♠	Pass

◇ Q led

South
♠ K J 10 6 2
♡ A Q J
◇ 8 2
♣ A K 7

Playing in Four Spades, you win the diamond opening and take the heart finesse, which loses. You win the diamond return and play a trump to the King. East wins the next trick with the Ace of trumps and you ruff the diamond return. The position is:

North
♠ Q
♡ 7 6 3
◇ —
♣ 6 4 3

South
♠ J 6
♡ A J
◇ —
♣ A K 7

If the hearts are 3-3 you can make an overtrick by cashing ♡ A J before drawing the last trump; but if the third heart is ruffed you will lose the contract. At this point you must consider what is likely to happen at other tables. Some North players, for sure, will respond 1NT to the opening One Spade and will finish in 3NT. Against a minor suit lead they will have to force out ♠ A and ♡ K and may lose four tricks before they can enjoy a second heart. So, in Four Spades, play safely for your contract.

4

LONG SHOTS AND SACRIFICES

In a popular contract the object is not primarily to make a specific number of tricks but to make plays that are odds on to succeed. In an unusual contract the approach is quite different. The declarer must decide where he wants to go and must follow his star, no matter how distant.

<table>
<tr><td></td><td></td><td>North</td></tr>
<tr><td></td><td></td><td>♠ Q J 9 7 5 3</td></tr>
<tr><td></td><td></td><td>♡ 5</td></tr>
<tr><td></td><td></td><td>◇ A K 7 4</td></tr>
<tr><td>South</td><td>North</td><td>♣ 8 2</td></tr>
<tr><td>—</td><td>1 ♠</td><td></td></tr>
<tr><td>2 ♣</td><td>2 ◇</td><td>South</td></tr>
<tr><td>3NT</td><td>Pass</td><td>♠ K 10 4</td></tr>
<tr><td></td><td></td><td>♡ A K 4 3</td></tr>
<tr><td></td><td>♡ 2 led</td><td>◇ 9 6</td></tr>
<tr><td></td><td></td><td>♣ A Q 10 5</td></tr>
</table>

The bidding is poor in several ways. Let us pass over that and admit that we are in a bad contract which perhaps nobody else will play. The question is, How can we out-score the popular Four-Spade contract? Unless trumps are led against Four Spades, declarer will ruff two diamonds and make twelve tricks. On a trump opening he may need a club finesse or a squeeze for the same result.

In 3NT it is useless to win the heart lead, drive out the Ace of spades, and settle for ten safe tricks. A finesse of the Queen of clubs will not help either, for if you make eleven tricks this way, everyone else will be making twelve. A squeeze in notrumps is barely possible. The best chance of avoiding a bottom score is to take the deep finesse in clubs and perhaps annoy everyone by registering 690.

Contracts may be unusual in the sense of being particularly good; declarer will then play safe, as at any other kind of scoring. Here we are considering contracts which are unusual because they are bad. A contract in the right suit may be unusual if it is manifestly at the wrong level. Some players imagine that if they have stopped short of a likely game they must play on the assumption of a bad break, hoping that pairs in the game contract will be defeated. There is a fallacy in this approach, as an example will quickly show:

North
♠ 8 4 2
♡ K 10 2
♢ A 8 6 3
♣ A Q 10

South	North
—	1 ♢
1 ♠	1 NT
2 ♠	Pass

South
♠ A Q 10 7 5 3
♡ Q J 6
♢ 5
♣ J 4 2

♡ 5 led

Defending against Two Spades, East wins with ♡ A and returns a diamond. Dummy wins and a diamond is ruffed. South suspects he has missed game and his depression is increased when a finesse of ♣ Q holds. He reflects that some North players will open One Club and some 1NT, and in either case game will probably be reached. The only hope, he tells himself, is to place West with ♠ K J 9 x. On this assumption he embarks on a trump-reducing play which has a chance of succeeding if West holds a 4-3-4-2 pattern but in most other circumstances is likely to cost a trick. Of course, the whole project is foolish, because if Four Spades is not on, South will get a good result automatically for not having bid it. The probable effect of his contortions is that he will lose matchpoints to any other pair that stays short of game.

One occasion when it may be right to play for safety in an unpopular contract is when you are hoping the field will be defeated in a different denomination.

North
♠ J 9 8 3
♡ 10 8 2
◇ A 8 4 2
♣ A 7

South	*North*
1NT	2NT
Pass	

♡ 4 led

South
♠ K 10 5 4 2
♡ K Q J
◇ Q J
♣ K 8 6

Had South opened with the normal bid of One Spade, he would surely not have stayed out of game in spades, which other pairs will bid. If Four Spades is on, it hardly matters how South plays, so he must assume it will be defeated and that a plus score will be sufficient. He wins the opening lead with the Queen of hearts and returns the King of spades. Declarer is willing to lose two spade tricks but cannot afford to cross to dummy for a losing spade finesse, opening up one of the minor suits.

WHEN THERE HAS BEEN COMPETITIVE BIDDING

On most competitive hands it is difficult to forecast the course of events at other tables. Declarer's aim should be to get as close as possible to his contract rather than carry his banner to outright victory or crushing defeat. Many players would take the wrong line on this sort of hand.

North
♠ Q 6 2
♡ K 5
◇ 10 8 7 6 3
♣ A J 4

♠ A led

South
♠ K
♡ A Q 10 8 4 3
◇ 5
♣ Q 9 6 3 2

South	West	North	East
—	1 ♠	Pass	2 ♠
3 ♡	3 ♠	4 ♡	4 ♠
5 ♡	Double	All pass	

When the dummy goes down you see that you may have misjudged the situation, for partner has good defence and your King of spades was not such a dead duck as you thought. After cashing the Ace of spades West switches to the King of diamonds and you ruff the next diamond. A finesse of ♣ J loses to the King and you ruff another diamond.

Now some players would apply a false test. 'If the hearts are 3-2,' they would say, 'we have made a phantom sacrifice. The only chance to emerge with a decent score is to play East for ♡ J x x x.'

The proper way to look at it is this: If we could have defeated Four Spades, then we must lose to all pairs who beat that contract. If Four Spades is on, we have done well already by sacrificing. Meanwhile, we don't want to lose to other pairs in Five Hearts. In particular, we don't want to lose 300 and be out-scored by pairs who lose 140 or 170 defending against a part score in spades. So we must play Five Hearts in the natural way.

In the next hand there is a sounder argument for relating your play to possible events at other tables.

North
♠ J 10 7 5
♡ 10 8 3
◇ J 10 8 6
♣ K 8

♡ K led

South
♠ A K 9 8 6
♡ 7 2
◇ 9 7 4 2
♣ A 5

With neither side vulnerable, the bidding goes:

South	West	North	East
1♠	Double	3♠	4♡
4♠	Pass	Pass	Double
All pass			

Against the sacrifice bid of Four Spades, East-West take two hearts and three diamonds, then exit with a club. Both follow to a round of spades. The problem is whether to finesse or play for the drop.

If trumps are 2-2, then South has made a phantom sacrifice and, as against tables where East-West are allowed to play in Four Hearts, it will make little difference whether he goes down 300 or 500. But if trumps are 3-1, minus 300 will be good, minus 500 bad. It is logical to play for the only situation that may produce a good score, especially as there is little to choose between the finesse and the play for the drop.

Be on the look-out for hands that have not been competitive at your table but which may well be so at others. On this deal both sides are vulnerable.

North
♠ A Q 5
♡ 10 9 6 3 2
◇ 9 7 6
♣ Q 5

South	*North*
1 ♡	3 ♡
Pass	

South
♠ 7
♡ K Q J 8 7
◇ J 10 3
♣ K 8 7 6

♠ 3 led

Having opened One Heart on a sub-minimum hand, you pass North's raise to Three. When West leads ♠ 3 the question is whether to finesse dummy's Queen, hoping to throw a diamond on the Ace and make the contract, or to play for one down.

You will be set two tricks if you finesse in spades and lose, but at rubber bridge the risk would be worth taking. At duplicate you should reflect that not everyone will open the South hand and in any case East-West, with 22 points and nine spades between them, will surely be less timid at some other tables than they have been at yours. Usually the deal will be played by East-West in a spade contract, which must be made. Therefore you should get a good board as long as you lose no more than 100 points. You must avoid being set 200, as some East-West pairs may score only 170. So put up ♠ A and concede 100.

WHEN YOU ARE DOUBLED IN A FREELY BID CONTRACT

Sometimes you will be doubled in a normal contract because the trumps break badly or the defenders are quick on the trigger, or because they are shooting for tops. You then have to estimate how many other players are likely to be doubled in the same contract.

North
♠ 6
♡ K Q 10 3
◇ A J 5
♣ Q 8 7 4 3

♡ A led

South
♠ A K 10 7 4 3 2
♡ J
◇ K 8 3 2
♣ A

South	West	North	East
1 ♠	Pass	2 ♣	Pass
3 ♠	Pass	3NT	Pass
4 ♠	Double	All pass	

West, who has doubled Four Spades, cashes ♡ A and switches to a club. When South leads a high trump, East shows out. If West holds the Queen of diamonds dummy's Jack will be an entry, enabling declarer to shorten his trumps by ruffing twice. If declarer can reduce his hand to ♠ K-10-x-x without sustaining a ruff, West can be end-played in trumps and the contract made.

However, this line of play is more likely to result in eight tricks than ten. The same contract is likely to be doubled at other tables, so South should play quietly for one down.

Rather more often, it will not be safe to assume that other pairs will be doubled. Should declarer then snatch at any chance to make the contract? Sometimes; but don't forget, during the play, that at tables where the contract has not been doubled, the declarer may be having a harder time. One down doubled will not necessarily be bad on this type of deal:

North
♠ J 6 2
♡ A Q 9 6 4
◇ 7 3
♣ A 10 5

♣ 4 led

South
♠ K Q 10
♡ K 5
◇ K J 9 6 2
♣ Q 8 7

South	West	North	East
1 ◇	Pass	1 ♡	Pass
1NT	Pass	2NT	Pass
3NT	Double	All pass	

East wins the first trick with the King of clubs and returns the 2. With a lead no better than J 9 x x x, West would not have doubled 3NT unless he held the diamonds well wrapped up. The sensible way to play the hand is to force out the Ace of spades first. Say that West wins and clears the clubs. Now cash three hearts, not expecting them to break, and two spades, planning then to duck a diamond to West. After making his clubs West will give you an eighth trick in diamonds. If the cards lie as you expect, this may be worth an average.

HOW TO PLAY SACRIFICE CONTRACTS

When you are in a clearly defensive or sacrificial contract, the crucial question is: What is the danger level and can you keep the penalty below it?

Suppose that, not vulnerable, you buy the contract for Three Hearts and see that the hand belongs to your opponents in a part score. You must direct all your attention to keeping the loss to 100. If you lose 150, that will be bad unless opponents can make ten tricks in spades.

At game level you can afford to lose 300 if opponents are not vulnerable, 500 if they are vulnerable. But that does not

mean that you can afford any precaution in order to keep
the loss below the score the opponents could have made. You
have to bear in mind that other pairs will be sacrificing too,
and you may win many points by 'getting out' a little cheaper
than they do.

At the slam level the same sort of arithmetic applies: to
save a vulnerable major-suit slam you can afford to go seven
down, not vulnerable, and so on. It is a sound principle not
to save against a grand slam unless you think it will cost you
less than the value of a small slam. Some pairs may not reach
the Seven level.

Here is an example of a typical sacrifice at game level
where the play would be influenced by the vulnerability:

> *North*
> ♠ 7 6 5
> ♡ J 8 4
> ◇ K 10 7 5 3
> ♣ 10 2

♠ K led

> *South*
> ♠ 4
> ♡ A K Q 6 5 3
> ◇ Q 2
> ♣ J 8 4 3

You are in Five Hearts doubled, defending against Four
Spades. The defence begins with two rounds of spades. Now
if opponents are vulnerable and you are not, you can afford to
go three down and must make sure of a club ruff by leading a
club at once. That should bring in eight tricks by way of six
hearts, a diamond and a ruff.

If the vulnerability is equal you can afford to go two down
only and must try to make some tricks in diamonds. You lead
the Queen of diamonds at trick 2 and have a number of
chances to arrive at nine tricks. If hearts are 2-2, one long
diamond will suffice; if they are 3-1 you may need the finesse of
◇ 10.

PLAYING TO THE SCORE

Many players attempt to estimate their score as they go along and become very proficient at it. Even if you do not estimate each board separately you can form an impression so that near the finish you can say, 'I reckon we are about 55%,' or whatever it may be. With a little experience you will be able to gauge your score within two or three per cent. If you overestimate one result you will underestimate another, and in the end you won't be far out.

In a typical pairs event—say a Howell with 14 pairs playing 26 boards—a score of about 60% to 63% will usually be good enough to win. In such an event the average for each board will be 6 (assuming that you score 2 for each pair you beat, 1 for each with whom you tie). It is not at all difficult to put down an estimated score for each board, ranging from 0 to 12. That will give you an idea, if you are in the running, how much you need to do over the last few boards. Suppose you play this hand in 3NT near the finish:

```
                              North
                              ♠ K 7 5
                              ♡ A 8 4
                              ◇ A 5 4
                              ♣ 8 7 4 2
       South    North
       1NT      3NT
       Pass                   South
                              ♠ A Q 2
                              ♡ K 10
             ♠ 3 led         ◇ K J 9 6 2
                              ♣ K 9 3
```

West leads a low spade in a manner that suggests this will be the normal opening. Suppose, first, that you estimate your score to be about 60% at the moment. In that case, you are probably leading and should be content with an average. Win the spade, lead a diamond to the Ace and finesse the Jack. If it loses, you are still safe for nine tricks. That is how most people will play the hand.

Suppose next that your estimated score is around 56%. In that case you will have to put on steam to win. In the vernacular, you must shoot for tops. One possibility is to play the diamonds in a way that is slightly against the odds—taking Ace and King instead of finessing. A more subtle manoeuvre is to win the spade lead in dummy and lead a club up to the King, as though clubs were your main suit. A number of things may happen. Even if West holds something like A x x or A J x in clubs there is an excellent chance that he will hold off—especially if he is a good player. If West puts on the Ace of clubs and returns the suit, unlucky!

5

MATCH-POINT DEFENCE

When the odds are right you are prepared, as declarer, to risk your contract for an overtrick. Sometimes, admit it, you take that kind of risk at rubber bridge too. But as a defender how often, for the sake of killing an overtrick, do you reject a play that might beat the contract? Somehow that is psychologically unattractive.

North
♠ Q 8 4
♡ 8 6
◇ A 10
♣ A Q 10 5 4 2

South	*North*		*East*
1 ♣	2 ♣		♠ A
2 ♠	4 ♣		♡ J 8 5 4 2
Pass		◇ K led	◇ 9 7 6 3
			♣ 9 8 6

East is defending Four Spades and dummy wins the opening diamond lead, South dropping the 4. When he comes in with ♠ A, a rubber-bridge player will return a heart; it is, after all, just possible that South has opened on ♣ K J 10 x x x and two Kings, or J 10 9 x x x with ♡ A Q and the King of clubs. At duplicate the correct return is a diamond, to make sure of the Queen, even though this resigns all hope of beating the contract. The chance of finding West with specific cards is not good enough to compensate for the more frequent occasions when declarer will hold ♡ A and scamper off with twelve tricks.

You often have to play that kind of defence at duplicate, for although in general it is right for a declarer to be acquisitive, defenders should more often set themselves modest objectives. Look for a play that is more likely to save a trick than to cost one, and do not let the fate of the contract be the only consideration.

This next deal, which occurred in the Masters Pairs, is technically more advanced but gives rise to the same kind of analysis. With neither side vulnerable, South reaches Four Spades. You are East and you win the first trick with the Ace of clubs, declarer playing low. What now?

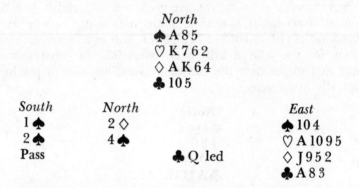

North
♠ A 8 5
♡ K 7 6 2
♢ A K 6 4
♣ 10 5

South	North		East
1 ♠	2 ♢		♠ 10 4
2 ♣	4 ♠		♡ A 10 9 5
Pass		♣ Q led	♢ J 9 5 2
			♣ A 8 3

At rubber bridge East would return a club without any deep analysis, for nothing more dynamic suggests itself. At duplicate you note that six spades and the King of clubs will give South nine tricks already. If he has three clubs and either red Queen, that will be eleven on top. If he has both Queens there will be a squeeze in the red suits for twelve tricks. On balance, therefore, it is right to lay down ♡ A at trick 2; on the actual deal this was worth a shared top, for South held ♠ K Q 9 x x x ♡ Q x ♢ Q x ♣ K x x.

A grasp of squeeze play is particularly important at duplicate. At rubber bridge a declarer does not play out a hand where the only possibility for an overtrick lies in finding an opponent with length in one suit and two or three key cards in another. At duplicate such chances must not be neglected. Equally, in defence, a player must be ready to cash any trick that is threatened by a possible squeeze.

Of course it is unwise to pass up a chance of beating a contract without considering what may happen at other tables.
When you are defending a contract that will give declarer a
fine result if he makes it, you try everything to defeat him,
just as you would at rubber bridge. In this respect the tactics
are similar to declarer's. Against a popular contract, look for a
play that will succeed more often than not, but against an
unusual contract, and particularly a doubled one, set yourself a specific objective and take risks to attain it. This next
deal holds a mirror to the tactics prescribed for declarer in
Chapters 3 and 4.

North
♠ Q 9 6 4
♡ Q 7 4 2
◇ 6 3
♣ 10 6 5

West
♠ A 10 5
♡ 6 3
◇ J 9 7 2   ♣ K led
♣ K Q J 8

South	West	North	East
—	—	—	1 ♡
2 ◇	Double	All pass	

For the moment we will not declare the vulnerability. East
deals and opens One Heart, South overcalls with Two Diamonds, you double as West, and all pass.

On the lead of the King of clubs East plays the 3. You switch
to a heart. Partner wins with the 10 and returns ♣ 2. You
win and play another heart, won by the Jack. East now plays
♡ K, South ruffs with ◇ 8, and you overruff with the 9.

From the play so far you place partner with ♡ A K J 10 x
and ♣ A x x x. You cannot be sure of the diamond situation
but are inclined to place declarer with A K Q 10 x x.

One point that will have struck you already is that both
Four Hearts and 3NT are on for you. Some pairs, perhaps the
majority, will play for game on your cards.

If your reading of the hand is correct, South has three
spades. If these are K x x you can exit with a club and be sure

of two down. That will be satisfactory if opponents are vulnerable and you are not. Suppose next that partner holds ♠ K x x. Then either Ace and another spade, to be followed by a trump promotion, or a club, leaving declarer short of a tempo to set up a spade winner, will lead to a three-trick penalty—good enough at equal vulnerability.

So far, you would be inclined to exit with a club, as that will work in either situation. But suppose you are vulnerable and opponents are not: now you must lay down ♣ A, for you can get 700 only if partner holds ♠ K J x and can lead a heart after the defence has cashed three spade tricks.

We remark at this point that doubles at a low level when vulnerable against not are almost always unwise unless game prospects look poor to the doubler. It is invariably difficult to pick up 700.

THE OPENING LEAD

At rubber bridge a defender goes for the lead most likely to set the contract; at duplicate, for the lead that is likely, in the long run, to produce most tricks. The distinction will be clear from the following examples.

South	West	North	East
—	—	1♣	1♡
1♠	2♡	3♣	Pass
3♠	Pass	4♠	All pass

West holds: ♠864   ♡A1085   ◇J9852   ♣3

The opponents have bid and supported both black suits and your side has overcalled in hearts. At rubber bridge, thinking only about beating the contract, you might lead the singleton club. If you find partner with the Ace you may be able to put him in again with ♡ K or ◇ A for a second ruff. At duplicate the danger that the club lead will present declarer with twelve rapid tricks is too great to be ignored. Be stolid and open with ♡ A!

Defenders at duplicate are more than usually averse to playing away from tenace combinations or unsupported honours. On the following hands West has to find a lead after an opening bid of 1NT has been raised to 3NT.

(1) ♠ 10 9 8 4   ♡ 10 5   ◊ A 2   ♣ K J 8 6 2

(2) ♠ J 8 4 2   ♡ 8 7 5   ◊ K Q 9 3   ♣ J 3

On (1) a club is likely to beat the contract if partner holds either the Queen or the Ace. A rubber-bridge player would look no further but at duplicate the approach is different: the 10 of spades, as compared with the 6 of clubs, will save a trick so often that it must be rated the better prospect. On (2) both spades and diamonds are too likely to cost a trick and the recommended lead is ♡ 8.

Short-suit leads against no-trump contracts are much more frequent at duplicate than at rubber bridge, but a slight problem arises in respect of the lead from three to an honour. Such a lead can be disastrous if partner reads it as fourth best, for he may lose both time and tricks in establishing a long card for the declarer. A third best lead is relatively safe when partner can work out that your longest suit has been bid by your opponents. The situation may be similar when opponents have used Stayman and given some indication of their length.

South	North
1NT	2♣
2♠	3♡
3NT	Pass

West holds: ♠ K 8 5 3   ♡ 10 8 4 2   ◊ A 10 6   ♣ J 2

Here the 6 of diamonds has a fair chance of striking East's length and is unlikely to deceive him. As neither major suit has been supported, East may well be able to place his partner with length there and so will be prepared for a short-suit lead in a minor. Similarly, when declarer has denied length in a major suit, a defender may be able to lead a deceptive fifth-best without misleading his partner.

We remark in passing that if, after a sequence such as that above, you decide to open a suit bid by an opponent, you are less likely to give away a trick by leading declarer's suit than by leading dummy's. Suppose you lead the 10 from K 10 9 x and find declarer with A Q x x, dummy with J x: you have lost a tempo, it is true, but that is all. If the length were in dummy you would have presented declarer with a trick as well.

MATCH-POINT TACTICS IN THE MIDDLE GAME

A defender who keeps abreast of the play will often realise, before declarer, that the contract is not at issue and that overtricks are what the struggle is really about. In such a situation declarer can sometimes be offered a chance to pursue the wrong war aims.

	North	
	♠ 10 7	
	♡ A 8 2	
	◇ J 9 7 4	
	♣ K J 7 3	

South	*North*	*East*
1 ♣	1 NT	♠ K 6 2
Pass	4 ♠	♡ Q 10 4
3 ♣		◇ A 10 6 2
	◇ 3 led	♣ 9 6 4

Defending against Four Spades, East plays the Ace of diamonds on the opening lead and South drops the King, doubtless a singleton. At rubber bridge it would not be dynamic to return a diamond, for if it suited him South would discard a loser, later discarding another loser on the established Jack. Rather than offer declarer that option, East would return a heart.

At duplicate East must take a more realistic view. South, after all, is likely to hold the King of hearts and then the effect of a heart return will be to drive him to a winning finesse in clubs. It is better to give him the chance to make an illusory safety play. This may be the full deal:

```
                        ♠ 10 7
                        ♡ A 8 2
                        ◇ J 9 7 4
                        ♣ K J 7 3
    ♠ 9 3                               ♠ K 6 2
    ♡ J 9 6 3                           ♡ Q 10 4
    ◇ Q 8 5 3                           ◇ A 10 6 2
    ♣ Q 10 8                            ♣ 9 6 4
                        ♠ A Q J 8 5 4
                        ♡ K 7 5
    ◇ 3 led             ◇ K
                        ♣ A 5 2
```

If East returns a diamond at trick 2 South will probably
discard a loser, taking the safe route to ten tricks and making
eleven as the cards lie. If he is forced to play the hand out
after a neutral return he will make twelve tricks.

One of the more subtle moves in defence is an underlead
where the defenders can judge that the declarer will not dare
to call the bluff. An underlead of A Q x or A J x is effective in
a situation like this:

```
                        ♠ K 10 5
                        ♡ 8 4
                        ◇ Q 10 8 2
                        ♣ K 9 6 3
    ♠ A J 4                             ♠ Q 8 7 2
    ♡ Q 10 7 3                          ♡ A 9 6 2
    ◇ J 9 5                             ◇ 7 6 3
    ♣ A 8 2                             ♣ J 4
                        ♠ J 6 3
                        ♡ K J 3
    ♡ 3 led             ◇ A K 4
                        ♣ Q 10 7 5
```

South	North
1NT	Pass

West leads a heart against South's contract of 1NT and
declarer wins the third round. A club lead is won by the King

and a club is returned to the Jack, Queen and Ace. West cashes the long heart, dummy discarding a club and South a spade. West's problem now is whether to underlead ♠ A, taking a risk that he may never make the Ace.

West must ask himself whether declarer, holding ♠ x x x, is likely to gamble by playing the King. As South has escaped a spade lead and has taken the winning play in clubs, the odds are that he will play for safety on the spade lead, accepting seven tricks. True, South could hold the Queen of spades, but in that case he will be missing one of the diamond honours and West will still make his Ace of spades.

The reader may be thinking, 'It must take West a little time to work all this out. If he leads a low spade after much pondering, surely South will suspect that he is underleading the Ace?'

That is true and it touches on a very important element of defensive play. A good defender must count the tricks as he goes along, pausing for thought *before* the critical moment; an 'advance trance', as it is known in the trade.

PART TWO

Tournament Acol

6

TUNING UP THE SYSTEM

In *The Acol System Today* the present authors gave an account of the best general practice in Acol bidding; what you might call the standard model of the system. Writing now for tournament players, and above all for regular partnerships, we wheel out of the factory the supercharged version, calling it 'tournament Acol'.

This first chapter looks at ways of increasing the efficiency of constructive bidding. The most revolutionary proposal is what we call the Economical Jump, which over a forcing response expresses two important features at one stroke. For the rest, there are some shifts of emphasis caused by the changed objectives of tournament play and, in later chapters, many new competitive manoeuvres. All these could well be regarded as part of tournament Acol. The sort of conventions that need specific mention on a player's convention card come later.

LIGHTER BUT SAFER

Light openings have always been a feature of Acol and are equally favoured by the successful Italian players, who have the additional advantage that they do not need to make prepared bids, as we understand them. This fast in-and-out style is surely best for competitive hands, the ones that decide close matches.

A later chapter contains an account of the Drury convention, which is designed to accommodate quite weak openings in third or fourth hand. Players who adopt this method will be able to 'open for a part score' more safely and more often.

There has been much controversy in recent years about the advantage or otherwise of restricting opening bids in a major to suits of five cards or more. This is certainly a playable method, especially in conjunction with a forcing 1NT response. It enables a partnership to play more often in a 5-3 fit and sometimes the immediate raise on three-card support will steal the contract. Against this, if you play five-card majors you have to open many more hands with a minor suit, easy to overcall, and in a competitive sense this is poor tactics.

Many Continental systems go further in the opposite direction, bidding a four-card major before a six-card minor. This so-called *canapé* method often gets good results. To bid that way at Acol would require major reorganisation, and we do not suggest it; the point we are making is that to stake an early claim to a major suit is good in principle. Thus there is no disposition to move away from four-card majors, as such. Where possible, however, an opening in a very poor major suit is avoided. Prefer 1NT, relying on the numerous gadgets available to help you finish in the right denomination.

RESPONDING ON WEAK HANDS

Acol players like to make a fast start but they don't keep a foot on the accelerator. In tournament play there is a definite move in favour of passing borderline responding hands, particularly when the natural response would have little or no pre-emptive value. Say that partner opens One Spade and you hold:

♠763   ♡Q82   ◇A732   ♣1065

A player who goes by the book may be inclined to think, 'I've got the minimum six points for 1NT, with a 10 to boot, and if partner is maximum there could be a game.' At duplicate, and even at team play, the fear of missing game is not so urgent and the danger of being defeated in 2NT, if partner raises, is more serious. A good rule for this and many other situations in constructive bidding is: When a move of any kind is likely to jeopardise a plus score, pass!

This is another type of marginal responding hand:

♠8   ♡K942   ◇QJ8542   ♣103

Over One Spade, 1NT is inapt, Two Diamonds is unsound, and a pass could also be wrong. At rubber bridge it would be a tricky decision. In tournament play there is the additional factor that opponents are more likely to reopen. You would welcome that, so the wise course is to pass.

The time to stretch a responding hand is when you fear, rather than welcome, the possibility of protective action by the opponents. Even a semi-psychic response may recommend itself in these circumstances. Partner opens One Diamond and you hold:

♠J63   ♡5   ◇107642   ♣8543

To pass would be to surrender, and Two Diamonds is more likely to help the opponents than to hinder them. Bid either One Spade or 1NT. In a pairs you needn't even look to see if you are vulnerable.

SECOND ROUND BIDS—FORCING OR NOT FORCING?

It is a fair proposition that when there are advantages either way, a tournament partnership should incline to treat a sequence as forcing rather than non-forcing. One reason is that the players will know how to benefit from scientific exploration. This has a bearing on two familiar sequences.

Reverse by opener after a response at the Two level. A reverse by responder has long been regarded as forcing, but what about a reverse by opener after a response at the level of Two? The modern tendency, which we support, is to play this as forcing on the grounds that if responder can bid at the Two level he will surely have something to say over opener's reverse; either he will have sufficient high cards for 2NT or a preference, or he will have a long suit in which he can make a minimum rebid.

With this established, opener has no problems on hands like the following, after One Diamond—Two Clubs.

(1) ♠AQ93   ♡A10   ◇KQ1084   ♣K6
(2) ♠AK4   ♡J6   ◇AQ1074   ♣Q42

On both hands bid Two Spades for the moment.

A return to responder's minor suit at the Three level, following a reverse, should also be forcing. Otherwise, after the same sequence of One Diamond—Two Clubs, it is difficult to develop a hand like this:

♠ A K 5 4   ♡ 6   ◇ A J 8 7 2   ♣ K J 4

You reverse with Two Spades and partner bids 2NT. Now the contract is still in doubt and Three Clubs, forcing, is the only good move.

Once it is accepted that the opener's reverse is forcing, a special meaning can be assigned to a jump reverse. After the sequence One Heart—Two Diamonds you hold:

(1)   ♠ A Q J 4   ♡ A K 7 6 3   ◇ Q 2   ♣ K 5

(2)   ♠ A J 6   ♡ K Q 8 5 3   ◇ A J 8 2   ♣ 4

On (1), although game is certain to be reached, bid simply Two Spades and decide further action after hearing partner's reply. On (2) bid Three Spades, a jump reverse, guaranteeing strong diamond support and showing an outside feature.

The raise to Four of responder's minor suit. How often, after One Spade—Two Diamonds—Four Diamonds, is it right to pass? Practically never, so it must be sensible to play the double raise as forcing.

♠ A Q 10 8 2   ♡ A 8   ◇ A J 6 3   ♣ K 4

The raise to Four Diamonds leaves space for cue-bidding. A jump to Five is reserved for distributional hands.

NAILING DOWN THE FORCE IN A NEW SUIT

A weakness in traditional Acol is that a jump-shift response to an opening bid is sometimes made on a strong suit, sometimes a weak suit, sometimes no suit at all. Suppose the bidding goes:

South	*North*
1 ♡	3 ♣
4 ♣	4 ♡
?	

South is in the dark both about the clubs and the quality of the trump support, for North is liable to turn up with any of these hands:

(1)   ♠ K 6   ♡ A Q 10 7   ◇ J 9 4 2   ♣ A 10 8

(2)   ♠ K 6   ♡ K J 4 2   ◇ A J 3   ♣ A 9 7 2

(3)   ♠ A 10 6   ♡ Q 8 3   ◇ K 4   ♣ A Q J 8 3

In tournament Acol only hand (3), containing a useful club suit, qualifies for a jump-shift. When partner forces, or when he makes a delayed game raise, you can rely on his having a genuine suit.* On all strong hands containing primary support for opener's suit but no biddable side suit, the new version of the Swiss convention is used (see Chapter 9).

INTRODUCING THE ECONOMICAL JUMP

When partner has made a non-forcing response to your opening bid it is not as a rule difficult to find a rebid that is at any rate satisfactory for the moment. Over a jump shift there is less space for manoeuvre, yet for some reason the best use has not been found for such bids as are available. After One Spade—Three Clubs, for example, what does *Four Diamonds* mean?

If the jump to Four Diamonds were made without prior arrangement one would take it to show good support for clubs and a control in diamonds. However, it is not particularly valuable in that sense. When partner has forced over the opening, the tricky hands to bid are those of limited strength which contain more than one feature worth showing. We suggest that such idle bids as are available should be used to portray this type of hand. The process is called the Economical Jump.

Our idea is that the jump over a force in a sequence like One Spade—Three Clubs—*Four Diamonds,* or One Spade—Three Clubs—*Four Spades,* should have this meaning:

(1)   There is fair support for partner's suit.

(2)   The opening bid is sound, but not far from minimum.

Author's note to second impression: It should have been made clear that this does not apply when responder follows the jump-shift with a bid of no-trumps.

(3)   When the jump is in the suit opened it shows a rebiddable suit; when in a new suit it shows a control.

We call the bid the Economical Jump because it conveys
those three messages in one bid.

South   North
1♠   3♣
?

South holds: (1)   ♠KQ1082   ♡AJ3   ◇J4   ♣Q96

Bid Four Hearts, showing a control in hearts as well as a
sound minimum and support for responder's suit. Remember
that in tournament Acol the force of Three Clubs guarantees
a genuine suit, so Q x x is 'fair support'.

(2)   ♠AQJ74   ♡42   ◇K84   ♣K62

Bid Four Spades. The suit is rebiddable and you hold no
first-round control in a side suit. This jump rebid used to
show a solid suit, but it seldom occurred and was never indispensable.

(3)   ♠AQJ4   ♡J5   ◇AQ10   ♣J873

Bid Four Diamonds. Here you have rather more than fair
support for clubs and better than a minimum hand, but the
E.J. tells more than a raise to Four Clubs and loses no space.
Over, say, Four Spades you follow with Five Clubs.

The next set of examples shows the E.J. in action after a
force at the range of Two.

South   North
1◇   2♠
?

South holds: (1)   ♠K63   ♡K5   ◇AQ10742   ♣54

Bid Four Diamonds, conveying the message of rebiddable
diamonds as well as fair spade support. In general, the opener
should incline to rebid a strong minor rather than show an
outside control. Note the difficulty of showing this type of
hand by existing methods: if South bids Three Diamonds on

the second round and North rebids Three Spades, a raise to Four Spades by South underplays the support.

(2) ♠ J 10 5   ♡ A 7 6 2   ◇ A Q 8 5 3   ♣ 4

Bid Four Clubs, choosing the lower of the suits where a control is held. Apart from the advantage in timing (room to bid Four Hearts over Four Diamonds), it is just as helpful to show singletons at this level as Aces; in a way more so, because partner can find out about Aces later by conventional enquiry.

(3) ♠ A 6 3   ♡ 4   ◇ A Q 8 5 2   ♣ Q 6 4 2

Bid Four Hearts. Here the traditional sequence, One Diamond—Two Spades—Three Spades—Four Spades, leaves the opener in doubt whether to continue. The singleton heart may well be the decisive factor in a slam.

Next, some hands where an Economical Jump would not be the best choice. The bidding has begun:

South	North
1 ♡	3 ◇
?	

South holds: (1) ♠ A 5   ♡ K J 10 7 6   ◇ Q 5 2   ♣ Q 5 3

This weak hand is not worth an E.J. of Four Hearts, still less of Four Spades. Bid Three Hearts.

(2) ♠ 10 7   ♡ A Q J 7 3   ◇ K 8   ♣ A J 10 4

This hand is too good for an E.J. of Four Hearts, which would limit the strength. Bid Four Clubs.

(3) ♠ A Q 2   ♡ K Q 9 5 3   ◇ K J 4   ♣ 7 3

Bid Four Diamonds. It is true that if you jumped to Four Spades you would still be in the saddle, but your mount might not be responsive, for he would assume a weaker hand. The E.J. is among other things an anti-trapping device, and to use it when you are already in the slam zone is in fact uneconomical.

No doubt the basic idea of the E.J. can be extended to many other sequences. Later in this chapter we instance some analogous situations after an Acol Two bid.

WHAT KIND OF NO-TRUMP?

If after an international pairs tournament you were to quiz the twelve leading pairs about their no-trump openings you would encounter every shade: 12 to 14 throughout, variable, three-quarters, strong throughout, and maybe the amorphous 20-point no-trump played by the winners of the 1966 Pairs Olympiad. The conclusion must be that there is not so much between one method and another as their various champions claim.

Acol players traditionally use the variable method, 12 to 14 not vulnerable, 15 to 17 vulnerable. There is nothing wrong with that for rubber bridge or for team play, but for duplicate the modern trend is towards the three-quarters no-trump— 12 to 14 except when vulnerable against not. Many players use a weak no-trump throughout, and as compared with the three-quarters-no-trump players they have logic on their side. Minus 200 is bad on a part-score hand whether your opponents are vulnerable or not.

When the 12 to 14 no-trump is played, rebids in no-trump after a suit response of One follow this pattern:

Rebid 1NT on 15-16 points.
Rebid 2NT on 17-18 points.
Rebid 3NT on 19-20 points.

If partner responds at the level of Two you rebid 2NT on 15-16. On stronger hands that are too balanced for a jump shift you go straight to 3NT. The fact that the rebid of 3NT has a rather wide range, from 17 to a barren 20, does not matter, for responder can give a quantitative raise to 4NT.

When this system of rebids is followed, the opener is committed to bidding 1NT on the great majority of balanced hands in the 12-14 range, at any rate in first or second position. Thus with ♠ 10 7 ♡ A Q J 3 ◇ K Q 10 5 ♣ J 6 2 he opens 1NT. If he opened One Heart and partner responded One Spade he would lack the points for 1NT and a rebid of Two Diamonds would be unsound on such a balanced hand.

A tournament partnership must attach meaning to all the sequences that may follow a 1NT opening, distinguishing for example between 1NT—Three Spades and 1NT—Two Clubs—Two Diamonds—Three Spades. This task, which is largely one of making the best choice of the many conventions available, is tackled in Chapter 9. For those who like to be up at the frontiers of knowledge, Chapter 11 contains a description of the Little Major sequences after an opening 1NT. There both Gladiator and Stayman are played.

OPENING 2NT

That reliable old work-horse, 2NT, has shown willingness to bear added burdens as the years go by. The diversity of conventional responses—Stayman, Flint, extended Flint, Texas—has increased the viability of the opening, so that nowadays it supports almost all 21-22 point hands that are not suitable for a Two bid. At present there is no better opening than 2NT on a hand like the following:

♠ 10 3   ♡ A K Q 8 6   ◇ A Q 10   ♣ A Q 4

Now that partners are more inclined than they used to be to pass a One bid, it is a mistake to open One Heart, and clearly Two Hearts may lead to a final contract of 3NT with the wrong hand playing it. However, the opening 2NT is not all honey either. Partners have a habit of raising to 3NT and putting down ♠ Q x. The next section, on Acol Two bids, includes a proposal that will make it possible to launch such hands more safely and accurately.

Conventions for use after an opening bid of 2NT are studied in Chapter 9.

TWO BIDS

The Acol Two bid exhibits something of a paradox. Like a warship of the old style, its presence is reassuring and affects the general strategy at many points not seemingly related; but when called into the actual fray it may prove both ponderous and vulnerable. Abandoning metaphor, we mean that if the Two bid were not available for strong distributional hands the fluency of many other Acol sequences would not be possible; but when called upon to act in person, the Two bid is not always impressive.

Two changes are suggested, the first both obvious and

essential. This is that Herbert responses should be played. With a weak hand responder bids the next-ranking suit instead of 2NT as at present. With the values for a positive he responds normally unless his suit happens to be the 'Herbert' suit; in that case he bids 2NT. One of the advantages is seen on the type of hand discussed in the last section:

♠ 10 3   ♡ A K Q 8 6   ◇ A Q 10   ♣ A Q 4

Acol players would be divided between One Heart, Two Hearts, 2NT, Two Clubs to be followed by a rebid of Two Hearts, and Two Clubs to be followed by 2NT. All have disadvantages. In terms of power and quality the hand is suitable for an Acol Two bid, but, as we noted above, Two Hearts—2NT is not a cheering prospect. At best, 3NT will be played by the wrong hand.

Clearly, Two Hearts is a much more satisfactory opening if the conventional weakness response is Two Spades. Opener follows with 2NT, not forcing, and if partner has three hearts and a ruffing value he will indicate support. We don't say that you will never land up in no-trumps with an unguarded suit, but you will be less likely to by-pass a better contract in a 5-3 major.

When on this type of hand the opening bid is Two Spades the bidding cannot be stopped in 2NT (any more than with existing methods), but at least the weak hand need not become declarer in no-trumps.

♠ A K Q 8 3   ♡ 10 3   ◇ A Q 10   ♣ A Q 4

Again open Two Spades. If partner gives the weakness response, Three Clubs, the best move for the moment is Three Diamonds. A response of 2NT to Two Spades will be equal to a positive in clubs.

One effect of using Herbert responses is that these strong semi-balanced hands, hitherto ugly ducklings in the Acol system, can be admitted with less reluctance to the clan of distributional Two bids. A no-trump contract is more likely to be played the right way up and sometimes it will be possible to subside in 2NT.

The new scheme of responses works particularly well on hands with diamonds and spades.

♠ A K J 3 ♡ 4 ◊ A Q J 9 8 4 ♣ A 6

Open Two Diamonds and bid Two Spades over the weakness response of Two Hearts. If partner then bids 2NT you say Three Diamonds, not forcing. That is better than bulldozing your way into 3NT via Two Diamonds—2NT—Three Spades—3NT. With five diamonds and four spades you may start the same way, with the alternative now of stopping in 2NT if partner shows no life.

The Economical Jump in response to a Two bid. Our second recommendation brings in the Economical Jump, expressing, as before, two aspects of a limited hand: in this case, fair support for the opener and a side suit of one's own. At present a certain type of responding hand can cause problems. Partner opens Two Hearts and you hold:

♠ 8 6 3 ♡ K 2 ◊ A J 8 5 4 ♣ 1 0 5 3

If you respond Three Diamonds and partner rebids Three Hearts, you may feel like bidding Four-and-a half Hearts, but you have to settle for Four Hearts. Now opener cannot be sure that you hold better than x x or a singleton Jack or 10 of trumps. A raise to Three Hearts on the first round, which in the system guarantees an Ace, may be a better move, but now you will not be able to show the diamond suit.

The fact is that in response to an Acol Two there is seldom room to show positive trump support and a biddable suit without going beyond the game level. The E.J. accomplishes both at a single stroke. On the hand above, responder bids Four Diamonds on the first round. Opener signs off in Four Hearts only if he has a minimum with no fit for diamonds. A bid in a new suit by opener will be interpreted for the moment as a cue-bid, though it may turn out that he has a two-suiter.

The E.J. in a side suit is essentially a limited bid, about 7 to 9 points. On stronger hands it will usually be better to make a simple response, taking control later. Minimum trump support for the jump is similar to the support for a direct raise—Q x, J x x or x x x if the rest of the hand is well adapted to suit play. The side suit should be at least K J x x or A 10 x x. When you hold the values for a positive response, but no side suit, express the hand by way of one or the other of the existing manoeuvres: either a single raise, showing trump support and an Ace: or a double raise, showing 9 to 11 points but no Ace; or a jump to 3NT.

Now that hands containing trump support and a side suit are shown by the Economical Jump, responder's worries are less in a situation like this:

South	North
—	2 ♠
3 ♡	3 ♠
?	

South holds: ♠ 10   ♡ A K 7 6 2   ◇ 9 8 5 4   ♣ J 7 3

Playing the old method, South would probably bid Four Spades, but with the uneasy feeling that partner might over-estimate the spade support. Playing the E. J., the raise is safe, for with positive spade support he would have responded Four Hearts on the first round.

SUMMARY OF THE NEW PROPOSALS

The reader may like a quick review of the main proposals made in this chapter:

Be willing to pass partner's opening bid of One on a barren or unsuitable 6 points.

Treat as forcing a reverse by opener after a response at the Two level (1 ◇-2 ♣-2 ♠).

Treat as forcing a raise to Four of partner's minor-suit response (1 ♡-2 ◇-4 ◇).

Follow the principle that a jump shift over an opening bid always denotes a genuine suit.

Over responder's jump shift use the Economical Jump on limited hands to show fair support for partner's suit plus either a rebiddable opening suit or a side control.

Play Herbert responses to Two bids.

When responding to Two Bids, use the Economical Jump to show a side suit and fair support for the opener.

7

COMPETITIVE MOVES IN DEFENCE

This chapter deals, not with 'detachable' conventions, but with understandings in the ordinary course of competitive bidding. The next chapter, Competitive Doubles, is on the same topic. Independent conventions are described in Chapters 9 and 10.

THE TRAP PASS DEMOTED

The Acol system of early defensive overcalls works well enough and the only observation we make about this phase of the auction is that the reputation of the trap pass has slumped in recent years. This is partly because there was an error in the original approach. Suppose South opens One Heart and West holds:

♠ 3 2   ♡ K 10 8 4   ◊ Q 7   ♣ A K 8 4 3

The family player bids Two Clubs happily enough, but the more serious contender remembers the warnings against overcalling on a moderate suit when strong in defence and opts for a trap pass. Now it is true that he might catch a cold in Two Clubs doubled, but the same could be said of many overcalls that are tactically right. The important point is that the opponents are more likely to commit an indiscretion if West overcalls with Two Clubs than if he passes. Deprived of the opportunity to respond One Spade or 1NT, North may raise to Two Hearts with less than normal support or he may hazard Two Spades on moderate values. From that moment, penalties are on the horizon. (It is true that players who demand good values for free raises and responses will avoid these perils; but one is prepared to leave them with that small negative success.)

The same sort of argument applies to take-out doubles when strength is held in the enemy suit. With neither side vulnerable the dealer opens One Heart and you hold:

♠ A 5   ♡ Q 10 7 3   ◊ K J 7 2   ♣ A 9 4

The text-books advise a pass because of the good defence and lack of preparedness for spades. However, we have noted that the Italians and others double freely on these hands, and having given this method a good run at rubber bridge we are convinced that it is superior to the trap pass. If partner responds One Spade the roof won't fall down; if Two Spades, you can bid 2NT. The worst that is likely to happen is that your left-hand opponent will bid at the Two level and your partner introduce spades on a moderate four-card suit; but remember, he has the Responsive Double at his command (see next chapter) and this will often give him an alternative to bidding a weak suit in an exposed position. Even if he does, the opponents may bid again.

The main tactical advantage of the double is that it will often prompt your left-hand opponent to overbid, attempting some sort of shut-out. By doubling sometimes with strength in the enemy suit, you keep them in a state of uncertainty that will extend to the play.

NEW ROLE FOR THE CUE-BID

Although the present system of overcalling is satisfactory, there is much scope, and much need, for innovation in the manoeuvres that follow. We look first at the problems of fourth hand after his partner has overcalled in a suit, examining the different situations that arise when third hand has passed, raised, or bid a new suit.

1. *When third hand passes.*

The chances now are quite strong that the deal belongs to the defending side. At present it is not easy for the fourth player to signify this: he lacks ways of making a purposeful entry into the auction.

South	West	North	East
1 ♣	1 ♡	No	?

What does a raise by East mean in this situation? According to the general theory of competitive bidding, the defending side is more often being obstructive than constructive. In our earlier book it was proposed that raises of a non-vulnerable overcall should be in principle pre-emptive, raises of a vulnerable overcall an accurate expression of values. But that is not satisfactory either, for the real problem, how to distinguish between different types of raise, is not solved. A defender should be able to raise pre-emptively in a situation like this:

♠ 85   ♡ Q 10 6 2   ◇ K J 8 7 3   ♣ 7 6

After an opening bid of One Club on your left and an overcall of One Heart by partner, you would like, with both sides vulnerable, to raise defensively to Three Hearts. But it would not be safe unless you could affix a tag, 'Stop now!'

The corresponding dilemma, when not vulnerable, is that you may lack safe means to suggest game if partner has a fairly good overcall.

♠ K J 9 4   ♡ J 8 5   ◇ A Q 6   ♣ 7 6 3

This time partner overcalls One Club with One Spade. You raise to Two, all your hand is worth if partner is 'operating'. But if it turns out that his overcall is sound and your diamonds are working, you may miss game.

The solution in both instances is to make more intensive use of the cue-bid in the opponent's suit. At present the cue-bid serves as a general-purpose force in various situations. We review these shortly, as none is excluded by the new method.

South	West	North	East
1 ♣	1 ♠	Pass	2 ♣

According to existing practice, East may hold:

(1)   ♠ K J 5 4   ♡ 3 2   ◇ A K J 10 5   ♣ A 4

This is the old-fashioned type of cue-bid—strong support for partner and control in the enemy suit. A slam is not out of the question.

(2) ♠105   ♡AK10   ◇AKJ42   ♣J106

This is a typical modern use of the cue-bid, allowing for a possible final contract of 3NT, or even Five Diamonds, as an alternative to Four Spades.

(3) ♠852   ♡AQ106   ◇AK2   ♣742

Here, after a vulnerable overcall, you would cue-bid Two Clubs and raise a rebid of Two Spades to Four Spades. Not vulnerable, you would follow with Three Spades, not entirely forcing.

It seems entirely practicable for the cue-bid, while continuing to perform the valuable duties set out above, to solve also the problem of intermediate hands. Let a cue-bid, in response to partner's overcall, promise at first no more than a sound constructive raise. Later it may or may not turn out that the player holds a stronger hand. For this reason we call it the Two Way Cue-bid.

It follows always—and this is the thread that runs through the whole of this section—that when fourth hand raises the overcall he is bidding defensively.

South	West	North	East
1 ◇	1 ♠	Pass	?

As East you hold:

(1) ♠J74   ♡82   ◇A854   ♣9632

Even if vulnerable, it is safe to bid Two Spades, known to weak.

(2) ♠Q10642   ♡8   ◇943   ♣K843

At any score jump to Three Spades, known to be defensive.

(3) ♠A982   ♡J4   ◇1032   ♣AQ75

This hand is worth a constructive raise to Three Spades, so first you should bid Two Diamonds.

The two-way cue-bid is just as valuable when partner has overcalled in a minor suit.

South	West	North	East
1 ♡	2 ♣	Pass	?

As East you hold:

(1)   ♠A4   ♡J75   ◇10863   ♣Q952

Raise simply to Three Clubs.

(2)   ♠A842   ♡75   ◇QJ63   ♣A54

Bid Two Hearts, meaning that you can support clubs and also that you reckon your side should win the part-score battle.

Next, we study the situation from the angle of West after East has made the cue-bid:

South	West	North	East
1♣	1♡	Pass	2♣
Pass	?		

As West you hold:

(1)   ♠J84   ♡KJ962   ◇K7   ♣976

With a minimum overcall you rebid simply Two Hearts. If partner bids a new suit, or no-trumps, you will know that his cue-bid was of the old style, a general-purpose force. If he raises to Three Hearts he will be showing the values for a sound double raise. On the present hand you will still pass.

(2)   ♠J6   ♡AQ8743   ◇A104   ♣93

With this more promising hand, if you had made a non-vulnerable overcall you would be worth Four Hearts now. Vulnerable, you would have less in reserve and a jump to Three Hearts would be sufficient.

(3)   ♠J5   ♡AJ763   ◇KJ104   ♣96

With a fair two-suiter you bid Two Diamonds and await events. If partner bids Two Hearts, you pass. If he jumps to Three Hearts, showing a sound raise to that level, you bid game.

(4)   ♠73   ♡AK1054   ◇AJ   ♣Q432

Now you are maximum in terms of high cards. You show this by bidding Three Clubs.

A further suggestion may prevent the wreck of many game

contracts. In the following sequence, how would you interpret the bid of Three Diamonds?

South	West	North	East
1 ◇	1 ♡	Pass	3 ◇

The jump in the enemy suit has no official status, but between keen bidders it would be held to indicate support for hearts and first-round control of diamonds. At best, this is a rare and not very necessary use. We think the bid should say instead, 'I can raise the hearts to at least the Three level, but the best game contract may well be no-trumps.' In the present sequence East-West may hold:

West	East
♠ K 4	♠ A 9 5
♡ A Q J 6 3	♡ K 10 5
◇ J 8 4 2	◇ Q 7 6
♣ 7 4	♣ A Q 8 3

The usual story on such hands is one down in Four Hearts after a diamond ruff, and the remark, '3NT is a make, but how can we bid it?' Over the jump cue-bid West, holding length in diamonds, will easily select the right contract.

Still dealing with raises of a simple overcall, we turn now to the situation where third hand intervenes.

2. *When third hand raises his partner's opening.*

South	West	North	East
1 ♡	1 ♠	2 ♡	?

After third-hand has raised the opening bid, East has a different tactical problem. There is not much advantage in pre-emption, so a raise of second-hand's overcall is in principle a value bid. Nevertheless, the two-way cue-bid can be used to inform partner that the hand contains fair defensive values. Suppose that in the above sequence you are East and hold:

(1)   ♠ A 9 8 3   ♡ A 6   ◇ K J 3 2   ♣ 9 7 6

With sound values for a raise to Three Spades you bid Three Hearts, the opponent's suit. If the opponents press on, West will not commit the side to a phantom sacrifice in Four Spades.

(2) ♠ Q 10 8 3   ♡ 7 4 2   ◇ K 9 7 5 3   ♣ 6

By raising directly to Three Spades on this hand you tell partner that the values are mainly distributional. West will know that he cannot rely on much defensive help against an opposition contract of Four Hearts.

The remaining situation is when third hand bids a new suit after the overcall.

3. When third hand bids a new suit.

As the opponents are not yet 'together', there may still be virtue in pre-emptive action by the defending side. Apart from that, by distinguishing between a distributional and a sound raise the fourth player helps his partner to judge up to what level to contest. In most sequences there will be room for East to make a cue-bid at the Two level.

South	West	North	East
1 ♠	2 ♣	2 ◇	2 ♠

East's bid of Two Spades, showing at least a sound raise to Three Clubs, is the same in effect as if North had passed.

In other sequences East will be able to cue-bid only at the Three level but will have a choice of suits.

South	West	North	East
—	—	Pass	Pass
1 ◇	1 ♠	2 ♡	?

Now Three Spades by East will be a self-confessed shut-out. With sound values for a double raise he has the choice between Three Hearts and Three Diamonds. He should prefer the suit in which he is stronger, for if South is semi-psychic 3NT may be the best contract.

A bid in an opponent's suit so often has a conventional meaning that it is difficult to convey the message that you actually want to play in a suit called against you. Turning now to a different department of competitive bidding, we offer a partial solution to that problem.

MAKING THEIR SUIT YOUR OWN

It is annoying, with a suit combination like K J x x opposite
Q 10 x x, to miss an easy game because an opponent has bid
an 'empty' suit such as A 5 3 2; still more annoying if he has
opened a semi-psychic on A x x.

The problem can often be solved by following this principle:

> *When one player has already shown a guard in an
> opponent's suit, a subsequent bid in that suit by
> either player is assumed to indicate a playable suit.*

Take the most common situation, where third hand opens
with, say, One Spade and fourth hand overcalls with 1NT.

South	West	North	East
Pass	Pass	1 ♠	1NT
Pass	?		

(We exclude, for the present, the possibility that East has
bid a 'Comic no-trump', as described in Chapter 10.)

Many players treat a bid of Two Clubs by West in this
sequence as Stayman, asking simply for the unbid major. We
suggest it be played as Stayman without the limitation. West
should bid Two Clubs when he holds *either* major suit and
the no-trump bidder, holding four spades, should rebid Two
Spades. With sufficient values to accept the game try, he may
even show five cards by jumping to the Three level.

That simple understanding, which does not increase the
conventional burden, will take care of many problem situations. The next suggestion will take care of a few more:

South	West	North	East
Pass	Pass	1 ♠	1NT
Pass	2 ♠	Pass	?

For the moment, East should assume that West is showing
a five-card spade suit and the values for 2NT. Thus a raise
to Three Spades will be natural, not a sort of responsive cue-
bid. If West has bid Two Spades on a different type of hand
altogether, that will become apparent on the next round.

This style accords with the recommendation earlier in this
chapter to lean away from trap passes. It is worth noting that

such passes are especially vain after a third-hand opening.
The opener, if under strength, will pass the response and then
fourth hand will have to make all the running with a puzzled
partner.

It is often possible to commandeer the enemy suit after
making a take-out double. The bidding goes:

South	West	North	East
Pass	Pass	1 ♡	Double
Pass	1NT	Pass	2 ♡
Pass	?		

As West has shown a guard in hearts he must allow for the
possibility that partner's bid of Two Hearts is natural. Thus
he should raise with four hearts. Lacking such support, he
makes some other descriptive rebid.

A familiar and important situation arises when third hand
bids a suit over the double.

South	West	North	East
1 ♣	Double	1 ♠	?

North's bid of One Spade may be genuine, may be a 'baby
psyche' on ♠ x x, or even a double-cross on a holding like
Q 10 8 x. There is at present a deficiency in the means of
countering. It is not unknown for East to double on K x x x,
West at some point to bid Two Spades on A J x, and grave
misunderstanding to follow.

This solution is proposed: (a) Double with moderate values
and as a rule only four spades. (b) Bid Two Spades, the suit
bid by the opponents, with a five-card suit and fair values.
(c) Bid 1NT, as at present, with a guard in opener's suit but
not necessarily in the suit bid by third hand. After the
sequence above East holds:

(1) ♠ Q 9 7 2   ♡ K 4   ◇ J 8 5 2   ♣ 7 4 3

(2) ♠ K 10 6 4 2   ♡ 10 5 3   ◇ 8 4   ♣ J 6 2

(3) ♠ K J 8 4   ♡ J 6   ◇ A Q 8 3   ♣ 9 4 2

On any of these, double One Spade. Hand (1) is typical for
the double. Hand (2) contains one more spade than partner
will assume but the double is still the best move on a hand

that is too weak for other action. Hand (3) is stronger than partner will expect and East will make a further move if the double is taken out. (Vulnerable against not, East should force with Two Clubs rather than double at the One level.)

Still with the same sequence:

South	West	North	East
1♣	Double	1♠	?

East holds: (4) ♠ K J 8 5 2   ♡ A 4   ◇ 7 6 3   ♣ 10 7 6

Bid Two Spades, promising five cards and fair strength. The bid is available for use in this sense because on other types the cue-bid can be made in the opponents' first suit. For example:

(5) ♠ 10 6 2   ♡ A Q 8 4   ◇ A J 8 5   ♣ 9 4

Now you bid Two Clubs, the suit called by opener.

Finally, we look at the critical situations that arise after an opening 1NT.

COMPETITIVE MANOEUVRES BY BOTH SIDES AFTER A 1NT OPENING

In this field the modern tournament player's tactics are markedly different from the rubber-bridge player's and are also an advance on his own manoeuvres a few years ago. One reason for this is the realisation, conscious or otherwise, that a double often leads to a poor result. One of the commonest entries on the score-sheet is 180, 280 or more, for 1NT doubled and made.

The double can go amiss in a number of ways. Sometimes partner takes out into your short suit; sometimes, having been informed on a previous occasion that you want your doubles left in, he passes on a yarborough and they make overtricks. Very often the contract can be beaten in theory but is made at the table because the best defence is not found. A simple fact, not generally realised, is that it tends to be much harder for the defenders to cash all their possible tricks in a low contract than in a high one.

It is wise to accept that the double is an unhandy weapon

and seek to contest the auction in a different way. In a pairs event, especially, the best strategy on semi-balanced hands is not to go after a penalty but to aim at your own best contract, using one of the conventions described later. If you find a fit you will usually score well, profiting from your knowledge of the lie of the cards. Taking a penalty is not the only way of extracting profit from an opponent who has laid his head on the block.

The best time to double is when you hold the lead and a long suit, a hand such as:

$$\spadesuit 5 \quad \heartsuit KQJ963 \quad \diamondsuit A106 \quad \clubsuit KQ4$$

The message is unequivocal: partner is expected to pass the double. With this understanding, you will also benefit when you hold the occasional giant.

In fourth position doubles are even less to be recommended. The enemy cards are now over you. If partner has a fair suit he may lack the entries to bring it in, and if he tries to find your suit he may pick the wrong one. In this situation a double begins to be safe only when you are at least as strong as the opener's maximum and are prepared for any lead.

Double by a passed hand. It follows from the last sentence that a partner who has passed originally can never have a sound double of 1NT. A good idea is to treat such a double as conventional, showing either a major or a minor two-suiter.

DOUBLING THE RESPONSE TO 1NT

As a competitive weapon, the double is much more necessary when third hand has taken out the no-trump opening into Two of a suit.

South	West	North	East
1NT	Pass	2 $\heartsuit$	?

A double by fourth hand will now be co-operative, showing a strong balanced hand. A double of a conventional Two Clubs is similar. In passing, it should be noted that the take-out by third hand stands in higher regard than it used to, precisely because it deprives the fourth player of the opportunity to make a conventional overcall.

The double of a suit take-out is also co-operative when third hand has bid over a double by second hand.

South	West	North	East
1NT	Double	2 ♡	Double

The double looks towards penalties but does not guarantee long trumps.

SEQUENCES FOLLOWING A 1NT OPENING AND A CONVENTIONAL OVERCALL

Most tournament players use an overcall of Two Clubs, and in some cases of Two Diamonds also, in an artificial sense. When these bids were first introduced their use was restricted to moderate and medium hands not strong enough for a double of 1NT. The tendency now, owing to mistrust of the double, is to use them on quite good hands as well.

Two of the more popular conventions (not always known by these names) are *Landy,* an overcall of Two Clubs which shows preparedness for both major suits, and *Ripstra,* an overcall of Two Clubs or Two Diamonds, which promises tolerance for the minor suit as well as length in both majors. In a more sophisticated convention, *Astro,* an overcall of Two Clubs or Two Diamonds shows a specified major and a second suit. All these and a further variation, *Aspro,* are described in Chapter 10.

For the present we consider the problems of the opening side when there has been a conventional overcall and the third player holds fair values.

South	West	North	East
1NT	2 ♣	?	
	(or 2 ◊)		

A trap pass by North may misfire, for East is not obliged to respond to the overcall. 2NT is best played as semi-defensive, probably based on a five-card minor suit. The way to show general strength is to double, not promising tricks in the suit of the overcall but saying initially, 'I have at least enough to contest the part score and am not prepared to let the opponents gain the contract cheaply.'

It follows that the no-trump opener should not let the double stand unless he has trump tricks.

South	West	North	East
1NT	2♣	Double	Pass
?			

You hold as South:

♠ K 8 5   ♡ A J 6 3   ◇ K 9 4   ♣ Q 7 2

Bid Two Hearts. East's pass, especially if playing the Ripstra type of overcall, suggests a fit in clubs, so it might be a mistake to pass the double.

REVIEW OF COMPETITIVE MOVES

The main recommendations of this chapter have been:

Don't rely on the trap pass as a weapon in duplicate.

When partner has made a simple overcall, treat all direct raises as competitive. With a sound raise, cue-bid the enemy suit first. Use a jump cue-bid to offer partner the choice between game in his suit and game in no-trumps.

When you or your partner have shown a guard in an opponent's suit, proceed on the basis that any subsequent bid of that suit is, or may be, natural.

When partner doubles for a take-out and third hand bids a new suit: (a) With four cards of this suit and limited strength, double; (b) with five cards and fair strength, bid Two of the suit.

AFTER A 1NT OPENING

Adopt one of the conventional overcalls of 1NT described in Chapter 10 and use it in preference to a double on the majority of semi-balanced hands.

In second position, double only when you may expect to beat the contract in your own hand. In fourth position, double only when you can stand any lead.

As a passed hand, use a double of 1NT to indicate either a major or a minor two-suiter.

In fourth position, double a take-out response on a strong balanced hand, irrespective of the holding in the suit doubled.

When second hand makes a conventional overcall of your partner's 1NT opening, double to show general values and a willingness to contest the part score.

8

COMPETITIVE DOUBLES

As a competitive weapon, a double has the special merit of consuming no space and leaving open every option. That is why we already have the take-out double, optional double, responsive double, and others. But although the uses of the double have been greatly extended, they have not been exhausted. In this chapter we study some further situations where a double can play a more effective role than that of executioner.

We begin by outlining the responsive double, not because we propose a new treatment but because it is related to the sort of manoeuvre we have in mind. This double used to be regarded as a special convention but by now it has woven itself into the system.

THE RESPONSIVE DOUBLE

When an opening bid is doubled for a take-out and the next player raises to the Two or Three level, a double by fourth hand is not primarily for penalties but shows willingness to contest.

South	West	North	East
1 ◊	Double	3 ◊	?

East holds: ♠ J 9 7 6   ♡ A 6 3 2   ◊ 9 7   ♣ K J 8

Instead of plunging for Three Hearts or Three Spades, or forcing with a bid of the enemy suit, East doubles Three Diamonds, indicating sufficient values to contest at this level. If

North had raised to Two Diamonds only, East would also have doubled, intending then to raise if West responded in hearts or spades.

It is true that there are times when the responsive double precludes the fourth player from doubling for penalties, but on balance the opportunities for chastening opponents who have over-extended themselves are not lessened. If the take-out doubler has a strong and relatively balanced hand he can always pass the responsive double, which guarantees some defensive tricks.

Responsive doubles used to be played up to the level of Three Diamonds only, but the higher the level the more awkward it may be to find a suitable bid, and doubles of Three Hearts and Three Spades are now also treated as responsive.

The doubles we describe in the remainder of this chapter also occur in the part-score range. They are available both to the opening and defending side. We call them 'competitive' doubles.

COMPETITIVE DOUBLES BY THE OPENING SIDE

Before using a double in any special sense one must be content to abandon the ordinary penalty meaning. So, a simple question: When can the opening side most happily dispense with a penalty double? Answer: When the defenders have found a fit at a low level. So this is the first example of a competitive double:

When both sides have found a fit, a double by the opening side up to the level of Three is competitive.

This provides a solution to one of the commonest problems in the game. The bidding has gone:

South	West	North	East
1 ♠	2 ♡	2 ♠	3 ♡
?			

With enough to bid again, South may be in a dilemma; or perhaps it would be more accurate to say that if South bids Three Spades, North may be in a dilemma. For what does

Three Spades mean? That South is willing to contest the part score or that he hopes to make a game? South may hold:

(1) ♠KQ1053 ♡94 ◇AQ107 ♣72

(2) ♠AQ962 ♡82 ◇AK74 ♣Q7

On the first hand South does not expect to make a game but he bids Three Spades because he is unwilling to sell out to Three Hearts. On the second hand he would also bid Three Spades, but now there are definite chances for game and had there been a pass on his right he would have made a trial bid.

The competitive double enables South to distinguish between the two holdings. With the first hand he bids Three Spades defensively. With the second he doubles, saying to partner, 'If you are not minimum we have a good chance to make Four Spades.'

Use of the competitive double by no means excludes the chance of a penalty. Consider this sequence:

South	West	North	East
1◇	1♡	3◇	3♡
Double			

South's double invites North to go for game in diamonds but sometimes North will welcome the chance to pass for penalties. In such sequences responder is much more likely than the opener to hold Q109x of the enemy suit.

Here it is the responder who makes the competitive double:

South	West	North	East
—	—	1♡	1♠
2♡	2♠	Pass	Pass
Double			

South holds: ♠74 ♡KJ8 ◇A642 ♣J1043

South is naturally unwilling to surrender to Two Spades and there may be a better contract for his side than Three Hearts. In this sequence 2NT by South on the second round might be regarded as 'unusual', fulfilling the same general purpose as the competitive double, but the double leaves open more options, including 2NT from North's side.

We turn next to sequences where the opening side has bid two suits.

When only the defending side has found a fit, a double by the opening side is competitive up to the level of Two-odd.

When the opening side has not so far found a good fit, a double is competitive only at a low level, for at the Three level a penalty double may be desirable. At the Two level the main purpose of the double is to secure partner's co-operation in making the next forward move.

Like an artificial bid of the fourth suit in a constructive sequence, the double tends to be the best choice only when no sound alternative is offered.

South	West	North	East
1 ♣	1 ♡	1 ♠	2 ♡
Double			

South holds: ♠ A 4   ♡ 7 6 4   ◇ K Q 8   ♣ A Q 7 6 2

The double says: 'I have no good bid available but we can do better than let them play in Two Hearts.'

In the next example the double is made by the responding hand:

South	West	North	East
—	—	1 ♣	Pass
1 ◇	1 ♠	Pass	2 ♠
Double			

South holds: ♠ 7 3   ♡ K J 6 4   ◇ A 10 8 5 2   ♣ Q 6

If a competitive double were not available, this would be a real puzzle. The same is true of the next situation:

South	West	North	East
—	—	1 ◇	1 ♡
1 ♠	2 ♡	Pass	Pass
Double			

South holds: ♠ K Q 6 4   ♡ 6 5   ◇ Q 9 6   ♣ K 8 4 2

Clearly, the competitive double is a happier solution than an uneasy raise to Three Diamonds.

Here the double gives a very good picture:

South	West	North	East
1 ◇	Pass	1 ♡	1 ♠
2 ♡	2 ♣	Pass	Pass
Double			

South holds: ♠ 6 2   ♡ A J 8   ◇ A K 6 2   ♣ K 10 7 3

South is not satisfied to sell out to Two Spades and his double expresses several features: better than minimum in high cards, limited support for hearts, diamonds not rebiddable. These inferences exist because, remember, the double is chosen only when no adequate descriptive bid is available. In the present instance North might be able to introduce a moderate club suit, which would fit well.

On the next hand the competitive double is a much better solution than a hoggish Three Hearts:

South	West	North	East
—	—	1 ◇	Pass
1 ♡	1 ♠	Pass	Pass
2 ♡	Pass	Pass	2 ♠
Double			

South holds: ♠ 6 3   ♡ A K 8 6 4 2   ◇ Q 10   ♣ 8 5 3

South wants to contest further. The fact that East's support was not immediate does not change the character of the double.

Here the competitive double occurs after the defenders have found a fit in their second suit:

South	West	North	East
1 ♣	1 ◇	1 ♡	1 ♠
Pass	2 ♣	Double	

North holds: ♠ 5 3   ♡ K J 7 6 2   ◇ A 8 4 3   ♣ Q 7

A final example of this type is presented from the angle of the doubler's partner:

South	West	North	East
1 ◇	1 ♡	1 ♠	2 ♡
Pass	Pass	Double	Pass
?			

South holds:

(1)   ♠ J 7   ♡ Q J 6   ◇ A J 10 4 2   ♣ K 5 4

Take out into 2NT, more promising than Three Diamonds.

(2)   ♠ J 2   ♡ A K   ◇ K J 10 6 3   ♣ K 7 4 2

You were not far from hazarding 2NT on the round before. Now you can expect some fit in diamonds and may reasonably venture 3NT.

(3)   ♠ 7   ♡ J 8 4 2   ◇ A K 7 5 2   ♣ A J 4

This is the sort of hand on which you would pass the double for penalties. The player who makes the competitive double is expected to be better than minimum in high cards. He might hold a singleton trump in this example, with 5-1-3-4 distribution, but even so defensive prospects must be good.

COMPETITIVE DOUBLES BY THE DEFENDING SIDE

The defending side has even less use than the opening side for penalty doubles at a low level. Take this simple sequence:

South	West	North	East
1 ♡	1 ♠	2 ◇	?

There is never much sense in a penalty double at this point. For one thing, the sequence is forcing; even if it were not, North having passed originally, a double to show good diamonds would be premature. It is surprising, really, that a more practical use for a double in this sort of situation was not developed long ago.

(a) *When the opening side has bid two suits.*

Because of the difference in status between the attacking and defending sides, competitive doubles by the defence occur in quite a different setting. They are made at the level of One or Two when only one member of the side has so far entered the bidding. The meaning varies according to whether the opening side has bid one or two suits. Take, first, the sequence mentioned above.

South	West	North	East
1 ♡	1 ♠	2 ◇	Double

East's double is 'competitive'. It expresses a combination of three features: tolerance for partner's suit, length in the unbid suit, ability to contest. The following would be typical hands for East:

(1)   ♠ Q 5   ♡ 7 3   ◇ A 8 4   ♣ K 10 7 6 4 2

(2)   ♠ 5 4 3   ♡ 6 5   ◇ K 8   ♣ A J 8 6 5 2

(3)   ♣ A 4   ♡ 10 6 2   ◇ 5 3 2   ♣ K Q 9 7 4

After the double East should allow his partner to plot the future course of the defence. If in the present sequence South rebids Two Hearts and West passes, the inference will be that West holds neither support for clubs nor rebiddable spades.

In the next sequence East doubles at the range of One:

South	West	North	East
1 ♣	1 ◇	1 ♠	Double

East may hold:

(1)   ♠ K 5   ♡ K 10 8 7 4 3   ◇ J 10   ♣ 6 4 2

(2)   ♠ 5 4 3   ♡ A Q 10 5 4   ◇ 8 6 2   ♣ Q 9

In either case it would be a trifle rash for East to bid Two Hearts freely, this being a higher suit than partner's. Where the fourth suit in the auction is lower-ranking than the suit named by partner, the inference of five-card length is not so strong. For example:

South	West	North	East
1 ◇	1 ♡	1 ♠	Double

East may hold:

(1)   ♠ 7 4 2   ♡ 10 5   ◇ K 8 6 2   ♣ A Q J 7

(2)   ♠A962   ♡J7   ◇1065   ♣KQ106

If East cannot find a call now on this type of hand he is liable to be shut out of the auction.

Here the double is made after the second suit has been supported:

South	West	North	East
—	—	1 ♡	Pass
1 ♠	2 ♣	2 ♠	Double

East may hold:

(1)   ♠63   ♡Q104   ◇KJ9642   ♣K5

(2)   ♠52   ♡K642   ◇AQ874   ♣93

If North had rebid Two Hearts in this sequence a double by East would have been for penalties. A double is competitive when a suit is raised, not when it is rebid.

(b)   *When the opening side has bid only one suit.*

The other main situation is when the opening side has bid and supported only one suit:

South	West	North	East
1 ♡	2 ◇	2 ♡	Double

Now it is possible for East to hold either (1) length in both unbid suits together with bare tolerance for partner's suit, or (2) length in one of the unbid suits and moderate support for partner's suit.

In the sequence above, East might hold:

(1)   ♠AQ104   ♡52   ◇103   ♣K8743

Now East will be happy to hear partner bid either black suit and he can stand a rebid of diamonds.

(2)   ♠K9652   ♡J4   ◇3   ♣AK932

This would be a problem hand under existing methods, for either Two Spades or Three Clubs might prove an unhappy choice. If, over the double, partner can only repeat his diamonds, at least he will find some high cards in the dummy.

(3) ♠A8753 ♡94 ◇1072 ♣K106

This sort of hand presents the player with a familiar dilemma: he cannot both show the spades and support diamonds, yet spades might be the best suit in which to contest. The competitive double gives West a chance to bid spades—three cards are enough. If instead he bids Three Clubs, East can amend to Three Diamonds.

SUMMARY OF THE COMPETITIVE DOUBLE

We present this summary in the form of a quiz:

OPENING SIDE

When is a double by the opening side 'competitive'?
At the One or Two level a double is always competive if the opponents have bid and supported a suit. If the opening side has also bid and supported one suit, a double is competitive at the Three level also.

What is the meaning of a double by the opening side?
Depending on the level, it will be a game try or just a 'push'.

DEFENDING SIDE

When is a double by the defending side competitive?
At the level of One or Two, when the doubler's partner has made a simple overcall.

What is the meaning of such a double by the defending side?
If the opening side has bid two suits, the double indicates length in the unbid suit and tolerance for partner's suit. If the opening side has bid only one suit, the double indicates either length in both unbid suits, with bare tolerance for partner's suit, or length in one of the unbid suits and moderate support for partner's suit.

Is a competitive double ever forcing?
No. Partner is expected to take it out, but he may pass for penalties.

PART THREE

Conventions

9

REVITALISING THE OLD

Conventions, like civil servants, are always with us and tend
to multiply. The object of this chapter is to brace up a few
indispensable veterans and pension off those no longer
needed. First, a group of conventions that are in the main
stream of modern bidding—the sequences after an opening
bid of 1NT.

CONVENTIONS AFTER 1NT

In the happy days when Two Clubs meant an assortment of
clubs, the only way to force over 1NT was to jump in a suit.
When the Stayman convention came into general use there
were two ways of reaching the Three level:

(1)	*South*	*North*	(2)	*South*	*North*
	1NT	3 ♡		1NT	2 ♣
				2 ◇	3 ♡

Players soon recognised the advantage of making a distinction between the two sequences. While the direct bid of Three
continued to be forcing, the jump to Three following Stayman
was classified as invitational. A little reflection will show that
this was the wrong way round. A responder whose only doubt
is whether to reach game in his long suit does not need to use
the Stayman convention; but a player initiating a forcing
sequence may benefit from the extra information supplied
by Stayman. Thus the modern tendency is to follow this
principle:

Direct suit bids over 1NT are weaker than a sequence reaching the same level via Stayman.

Observe how easily this works:

Direct suit responses, Two Diamonds, Two Hearts and Two Spades, are weak.

Direct jump responses in any suit invite game but are not forcing. Over a weak 1NT responder would jump to Three of the major on:

(1) ♠9 ♡KJ9654 ♢A852 ♣Q6

(2) ♠QJ87532 ♡4 ♢K3 ♣Q72

As is clear from the examples, the opener is offered a choice between passing and raising the major suit; there will seldom be much point in his rebidding 3NT.

A direct jump to Three of a minor is also invitational but now the opener's choice is between passing and bidding 3NT. The response is made when it looks as though 3NT will depend on bringing in the minor suit. Partner opens 1NT (weak) and you hold:

(1) ♠74 ♡A4 ♢A108653 ♣Q97

(2) ♠A96 ♡52 ♢K8 ♣Q108642

Respond with a jump to Three in the long minor. As a rule, opener should bid 3NT when he is not minimum and has three cards of the minor suit; should pass when he has a doubleton no better than Qx.

After Stayman has been used, second-round responses at the Two level are not by definition encouraging, but they should not be minimum.

South	North
1NT	2♣
2♢	2♡

Here there is an inference that responder could have sustained a rebid of Two Spades, and at least a possibility that he would have raised a rebid of Two Hearts. Some players, it is true, like to use Stayman as an escape hatch on very weak hands, but the advantage is uncertain, especially against opponents who know the right counter. On balance, it is better to retain the inference that delayed bids of Two Hearts and Two Spades offer competitive possibilities and may even be raised on a maximum.

Responses at the Three level, following Stayman, are forcing. The opener assumes for the moment that he is being offered a choice between game in the suit and game in no-trumps. The responder may of course have loftier ambitions; so the opener, when supporting the suit, should not fail to indicate whether his hand appears suitable for slam.

	South	North
	1NT	2♣
	2♠ (or 2♢)	3♡
	?	

South holds:

(1) ♠ K 10 5 2   ♡ K 9 8   ♢ K 6   ♣ A 9 7 2

(2) ♠ J 5   ♡ Q J 8   ♢ K J 7 3   ♣ K Q 6 2

On (1) South bids Four Clubs, an advance cue-bid. On (2) he simply raises to Four Hearts.

When responder bids a minor suit at the Three level after using Stayman, he shows good values and at least a five-card suit.

(1)	South	North	(2)	South	North
	1NT	2♣		1NT	2♣
	2♢	3♢		2♡	3♣

Three Clubs in the second sequence was at one time played as a sign-off. In the scheme we are presenting, both Three Clubs and Three Diamonds are forcing. (When partner opens 1NT and you hold a weak hand with long clubs, simply pass. Defensively, that is as good as anything.)

Over Three of a minor suit in that sort of sequence, Three of a major by opener is a no-trump probe, not a slam try. Suppose that in the first sequence above South holds:

♠ 1084   ♡ K Q 9   ♢ Q 74   ♣ A J 3 2

Over Three Diamonds he bids Three Hearts, proclaiming a guard in the suit.

Direct responses at the Four level. A jump to Four Hearts or Four Spades over 1NT is natural and limited. A jump to Four Clubs or Four Diamonds requests partner to rebid Four Hearts or Four Spades respectively (South African Texas). The object is to place the declaration in the hand of the no-trump bidder. Partner opens 1NT (weak) and you hold:

(1)   ♠Q J 107432   ♡5   ◇K4   ♣A J 3

(2)   ♠43   ♡A Q 10742   ◇J4   ♣A85

On (1) you are happy to be declarer, so you bid a direct Four Spades. On (2) it must be better to put partner at the wheel, so you bid Four Clubs, requesting transfer to Four Hearts. The use of South African Texas excludes the Gerber Four Clubs, asking for Aces, but the loss is negligible as there are other ways of obtaining the information.

Four-level bids after Stayman. The responder can use a second-round bid of Four Clubs or Four Diamonds to explore slam possibilities in a minor (Sharples convention), indicating specifically a four-card minor suit and at least the values for a natural raise to 4NT.

South	North
1NT	2♣
2◇ (or 2♡, 2♠)	4◇

North's bid of Four Diamonds denotes a four-card suit. The message is: 'If you have a fit for diamonds, slam should be there. If not, we will be safe in 4NT.'

There remains a jump to Four of a major after Stayman:

South	North
1NT	2♣
2◇ (or 2♠)	4♡

This sequence, oddly neglected, can be played as a slam suggestion, with emphasis on a strong trump suit. North may hold:

(1) ♠K5 ♡KQ108753 ◇AJ4 ♣3

(2) ♠A4 ♡AKQ872 ◇K643 ♣2

If South has opened 1NT with a poor holding in hearts he knows that he need not worry on that account.

SUMMARY OF RESPONSES TO 1NT

(a) *Direct*

2◇, 2♡, 2♠	Weak.
3♣, 3◇, 3♡, 3♠	Invitational.
4♣, 4◇	Texas.
4NT	Natural.

(b) *Following Stayman*

2♡, 2♠	Limited, but not minimum.
3♣, 3◇, 3♡, 3♠	Forcing, five-card suit.
4♣, 4◇	Slam suggestion, four-card suit.
4♡, 4♠	Slam suggestion, strong trumps.
4NT	Conventional (Blackwood or Roman Blackwood).

CONVENTIONS AFTER 2NT

Here the use of two conventional responses, Three Clubs and Three Diamonds, makes it possible to convey many shades of meaning. The basic system is Three Clubs Stayman, Three Diamonds Flint, Three Hearts and Three Spades natural and variable. We look first at the natural responses.

Direct bids of Three Hearts and Three Spades over 2NT offer, in the first place, a choice between 3NT and game in the suit. Responder may be weak or strong. When the opener holds three trumps and 'tops' he must not neglect to bid a new suit at the Four level as 'conditional acceptance' of a slam try. This possibility may have a bearing on the choice of first response to 2NT.

(1) ♠A853 ♡K10754 ◇Q42 ♣7

The best response to 2NT is Three Hearts, not Three

Clubs. Opener's rebid over Three Clubs will not take you much further; what you want to hear is an encouraging move over Three Hearts.

(2) ♠ A J 10 6 4 2   ♡ 5   ◇ Q 10 5 3   ♣ Q 6

Bid Three Spades, hoping for conditional acceptance. If opener bids 3NT you press on with Four Spades. This is not a minimum sequence and partner may bid again if a doubleton in spades was the reason for his sign-off of 3NT.

Direct bids of Four Hearts and Four Spades are minimum game bids. They are infrequent, for on most weak hands it will be better to employ Texas and let partner be declarer.

Direct bids of Four Clubs and Four Diamonds are Texas, requesting opener to rebid Four Hearts and Four Spades respectively. They may be used either on weak hands or when responder intends to bid on.

(1) ♠ J 86542   ♡ 763   ◇ A 6   ♣ J 4

(2) ♠ A 86   ♡ K 10 7 5 4 3   ◇ Q 4   ♣ 10 7

On the first hand respond Four Diamonds and pass Four Spades. On the second, respond Four Clubs and over Four Hearts bid Four Spades, a cue-bid.

Three Clubs over 2NT is usually described as Stayman, but the opener's rebids do not follow the same pattern as after 1NT. Instead, both players bid their lowest-ranking four-card suits until a fit is found or 3NT is reached.

	(1) South	North		(2) South	North
	2NT	3♣		2NT	3♣
	3◇	3♡		3♡	3♠
	3♠	3NT		4♠	

In (1) South's Three Diamond bid shows a genuine suit and does not exclude the possibility of a four-card major. In (2) a spade fit is found; note, however, that opener's raise to Four Spades is discouraging, to the extent that he did not make an advance cue-bid in one of the three suits.

The sequence 2NT—Three Clubs—3NT means that the opener's only suit is clubs. Responder may place sufficient reliance on this inference to jump to Six Clubs with only a four-card suit.

The search for a 4-4 fit ends at 3NT and bids of a minor suit at the Four level are natural, indicating length.

South	North
2NT	3♣
3♠	4♣ (or 4 ◇)

North's Four Clubs suggests a five-card suit at least. (He may possibly hold good support for spades, but that will appear later.)

A slight problem arises when responder holds a two-suiter with long clubs, such as:

♠6   ♡A8642   ◇7   ♣QJ8743

To bid clubs first and follow with Four Hearts would not be clear in some sequences, so it is better to bid the higher suit first. Later, if clubs are bid twice, opener must allow for the possibility that they may be the longer suit.

Three Diamonds over 2NT, the Flint convention, has undergone many extensions. The main idea is to enable the partnership to stop in a major suit at the Three level. Partner opens 2NT and you hold:

♠842   ♡J87432   ◇652   ♣9

You respond Three Diamonds, requesting opener to bid Three Hearts, which you intend to pass. If you had the same hand with spades instead of hearts you would transfer Three Hearts to Three Spades, expecting the opener to pass this.

The convention quickly became popular, but the 2NT opener tended to complain that he was hamstrung. Say that this is the opening hand:

♠A5   ♡KQ65   ◇AK7   ♣AQ85

Over 2NT partner responds Three Diamonds. You are ready to take your chance on game if partner has a heart suit and thirteen cards, but you know that if you bid Three Hearts he may pass. To bid Four Hearts yourself is risky because his actual suit may well be spades. The solution lies in Extended

Flint. With a hand of this general strength, opener can proceed as follows:

With strong support for hearts, bid Three Spades. Responder can pass or bid Four Hearts.

With strong support for spades, bid Three Hearts, as at present. If responder converts to Three Spades you raise to Four.

With strong support for both major suits, bid 3NT, inviting partner to name the suit.

And when the responder to 2NT holds a diamond suit? The simplest rule to follow is that if on the second round responder makes any bid inconsistent with the Flint convention, he has diamonds and is bidding naturally.

(1)	*South*	*North*		(2)	*South*	*North*
	2NT	3 ◇			2NT	3 ◇
	3 ♡	3NT			3 ♡	4 ♡

In the first sequence North has a diamond suit and obviously he is prepared for a higher contract than 3NT. In the second sequence he has a two-suiter with diamonds and hearts.

SUMMARY OF SEQUENCES AFTER 2NT

Responses

3 ♣   Both players show four-card suits upwards. Subsequent Four Clubs or Four Diamonds by responder is natural.

3 ◇   Flint, asking opener to bid Three Hearts. With maximum support for hearts opener may bid Three Spades, or with maximum in both majors, 3NT.

3 ♡, 3 ♠   Unlimited. If the suit is repeated over a rebid of 3NT, the responding hand must be good.

4 ♣, 4 ◇   Texas.

4 ♡, 4 ♠   Minimum game bids.

CONVENTIONS AFTER 3NT

An opening 3NT at Acol is made on a solid minor suit and, presumptively, no outside strength. When he does not want to stand 3NT, responder normally takes out into Four Clubs.

That is as far as the convention goes in Acol, but some further understandings developed in the Little Major merit inclusion. The most valuable addition is Four Diamonds, asking opener to name any singleton. With a singleton heart or spade opener bids the suit; with a singleton in the other minor he bids Five of his actual suit; with no singleton he bids 4NT.

(1) ♠AKQ10 ♡QJ632 ◇AQ ♣86

(2) ♠A94 ♡AK ◇J5 ♣AJ7432

With either hand bid Four Diamonds over 3NT. On (1) you are interested in a singleton heart; on (2) you can bid Seven Diamonds if opener rebids Five Diamonds, showing a singleton club.

Other understandings are as follows: 4NT is a generalised slam invitation, Five Clubs means that the hand is playable in opener's suit at the Five level, and Five Diamonds is to play (on a hand where responder can tell that partner's suit is diamonds and sees advantage in playing the contract from his own side).

THE SWISS CONVENTION

We turn now to conventions that follow an opening suit bid. In the well-established Swiss convention the comparatively idle bids of Four Clubs and Four Diamonds are used to express sound, as opposed to distributional, raises to game of partner's major-suit opening. Thus One Heart—Four Hearts is pre-emptive, One Heart—Four Clubs promises better values, and One Heart—Four Diamonds, in most versions, is stronger still.

Various meanings have been assigned to the responses of Four Clubs and Four Diamonds. Rather than use the convention in a restricted sense to show specific holdings, we suggest extending it to hands worth more than game and giving it a place in a comprehensive scheme that covers every grade of strong supporting hand. There are six general classes of supporting hand. After your partner has opened One Heart, this is how you express the various types:

(1) *A distributional raise.*

    ♠5 ♡KJ762 ◇Q10864 ♣73

    ♠Q8 ♡KQ104 ◇J97642 ♣3

As at present, you raise directly to Four Hearts.

(2) *The values for a raise to game, including a fair side suit.*

    ♠6 ♡QJ94 ◇A10762 ♣KJ3

    ♠J4 ♡A1086 ◇8 ♣AQ9642

Respond with a minimum bid in the side suit and, over any neutral rebid by partner, jump to Four Hearts on the next round. This is the technique of the delayed game raise. A reasonably good suit is promised.

(3) *A sound raise to game, but no side suit.*

    ♠AQ5 ♡J932 ◇A85 ♣K64

    ♠A4 ♡KJ73 ◇J7532 ♣A8

    ♠K62 ♡AJ753 ◇4 ♣Q954

Now use the Swiss convention. Respond Four Clubs and pass a rebid of Four Hearts.

(4) *A stronger hand, still with no side suit but worth a slam investigation if opener holds more than a minimum.*

    ♠K6 ♡KQ74 ◇A853 ♣Q43

    ♠Q1076 ♡AJ8643 ◇4 ♣K9

Respond Four Diamonds, still intending to pass a minimum rebid of Four Hearts.

(5) *A hand worth a slam try opposite a minimum opening, but with no side suit.*

♠A6 ♡AK106 ♢K954 ♣K102

♠AQ3 ♡KQJ2 ♢J8642 ♣A

Use 'double-barrelled Swiss': respond Four Clubs and make a further try over a minimum rebid.

(6) *A hand containing strong support and a fair side suit.*

♠KQ6 ♡KJ87 ♢AQ1082 ♣7

Make the normal jump-shift, with the useful understanding, as set out in Chapter 6, that a force followed by support for partner guarantees a genuine suit.

The special role of the Swiss convention in this scheme is to take care of the comparatively balanced hands that in the past have been difficult to express. This is better than using the convention to show specific controls. Four Clubs and Four Diamonds become members of the company instead of guest artists.

We do not want to overcrowd the canvas, but we remark in passing that these Swiss bids can also be used by the opener in a sequence like One Heart—One Spade—Four Clubs. Here Four Clubs would be analogous to Four Clubs over an opening bid, distinguishing between distributional and 'value' raises.

SWISS FOR THE MINOR SUITS

Hands that are strong in support of partner's minor suit are actually more difficult to express than hands worth a raise to game in a major. Partner opens One Club and you hold:

(1) ♠9853 ♡A108 ♢K7 ♣KQJ3

(2) ♠AQ8 ♡K5 ♢973 ♣AJ632

(3) ♠J752 ♡AJ7 ♢4 ♣AQ1073

It is difficult to express the value of these hands without going beyond 3NT. One Club—Three Clubs is not forcing at Acol, nor are such sequences as One Club—One Heart—1NT—Three Clubs, or One Club—One Heart—Two Hearts—Three Clubs. On the first two examples above it is usual to respond 3NT, which may be quite the wrong contract.

The Swiss convention can well be extended to deal with these hands. Over One Club a jump to Three Diamonds or Three Hearts, and over One Diamond a jump to Three Hearts or Three Spades, is equivalent to Four Clubs or Four Diamonds over One Heart or One Spade. On all three hands above the response would be Three Diamonds. (The loss of this bid in its present pre-emptive sense is easily borne, for it is seldom helpful to pre-empt in a new suit when partner has opened the bidding.)

Here partner opens One Diamond and you hold:

(1)   ♠74   ♡AQ   ◇AK753   ♣10642

(2)   ♠A62   ♡763   ◇AQJ6   ♣K94

On either hand respond Three Hearts, indicating that you are too good for a raise to Three Diamonds but have no suit worth calling.

(3)   ♠AQ3   ♡42   ◇AQ863   ♣K105

(4)   ♠K5   ♡J952   ◇AK74   ♣A85

This time respond Three Spades, showing a still stronger hand.

While setting out these Swiss variations we have not paused to consider the rebids by responder to Swiss. Obviously a rebid of the major at game level, in a sequence like One Heart—Four Clubs—Four Hearts, is a sign-off. If the opener bids Four Diamonds over Four Clubs that is a generalised slam invitation, without reference to his holding in diamonds.

OTHER ESTABLISHED CONVENTIONS

For the sake of completeness, it should be added that such widely played conventions as the Lightner double, the Unusual no-trump, the S.O.S. redouble, and 2NT over a take-out double (to express a sound raise to Three of partner's major-suit opening), remain part of tournament Acol. We have but few comments to make on these.

The Lightner double, traditionally asking for an unexpected lead against a slam, has been extended by many players to cover doubles of game contracts in some situations.

South	West	North	East
—	—	1 ◇	1 ♡
1 ♠	Pass	2 ♠	Pass
4 ♠	Pass	Pass	Double
All pass			

The double by a player who made a simple overcall must be rated as unexpected, and West should lead a diamond or a club—not a heart. (Of course, if West held five trumps, or a void in trumps, he would place a different interpretation on the double.)

In the field of the *Unusual no-trump,* there is some diversity about the meaning of an immediate 2NT over an opening bid of One. In the earlier book on Acol this overcall was described as natural, though probably based on a long suit. It is more in accordance with modern practice to treat the overcall as 'unusual'.

S O.S. redoubles occur at any low level when it is reasonable to suppose that if the player were satisfied with the doubled contract he would pass.

South	West	North	East
1 ♡	2 ◇	Double	Redouble

East's redouble is for a rescue and the suit bid by the opponents, hearts, is among the retreats open to West. This kind of redouble used to be known as the Kock-Werner redouble, but there is really no reason to give it a separate classification from an S.O.S. redouble made by the player who has been doubled.

Defence to Three Bids. Most players have arrived at their own solution to this difficult problem. In *The Acol System Today* we recommended the method known as x-3-x, where 3NT is the take-out request over Three Hearts and Spades by the right-hand opponent, 'double' in all other situations. Some players prefer x-4-x, where Four Clubs is the take-out bid over Three Spades. There is also a movement towards the American style, where double is always for take-out. For our money, x-3-x is as good as anything.

SUMMARY OF CHANGES IN ESTABLISHED CONVENTIONS

(Changes after opening bids of 1NT and 2NT are summarised *in situ.*)

Swiss convention. Use Four Clubs to indicate a sound raise with no side suit, Four Diamonds a stronger hand, also with no side suit. With a hand worth a slam try, containing no side suit, respond Four Clubs and bid again over any rebid.

Extend Swiss to the minor suits, bidding Three Diamonds and Three Hearts over One Club, Three Hearts and Three Spades over One Diamond.

Lightner double. Extend the principle to freely bid game contracts.

Unusual no-trump. Treat an immediate overcall of 2NT as 'unusual'.

10

BRINGING IN THE NEW

In this chapter we present what we believe to be the best versions of some modern ideas, most of them new to Acol. They occur in the following sectors of bidding:

> Slam enquiry
> No-trump overcalls
> Cue-bid overcalls
> Weak openings in third and fourth position
> (Modified Drury)
>
> Contesting against 1NT (mainly Aspro)

We begin with two forms of slam enquiry, the Roman Blackwood 4NT and the Trump Asking Bid.

THE NEW ROMAN

Most tournament players who seek to improve on old-fashioned Blackwood incline nowadays towards Roman Blackwood. In the most popular variation the responses to 4NT are:

Five Clubs	0 or 3 Aces
Five Diamonds	1 or 4 Aces
Five Hearts	2 Aces of the same colour
Five Spades	2 Aces of the same rank
5NT	2 'odd' Aces (hearts-clubs or diamonds-spades)

This schedule is definitive in the sense that a player holding one Ace can always identify two Aces shown by his partner. The word 'CRO', standing for Colour, Rank, Odd, will serve as a reminder of the order in which two Aces are shown.

The Five Spade and 5NT responses to Roman Blackwood take the bidding a step or two higher than normal Blackwood. This is not serious provided an economical method of asking for Kings is adopted. Say that the response to 4NT is Five Diamonds: then the next suit, provided it is not the intended trump suit, is an enquiry for Kings, with responses on the same principle as above (one step, 0 or 3; two steps, 1 or 4, and so on). If the 'next suit' is a possible trump suit and so not available for this purpose, then 5NT asks for Kings.

Indicating a void. An idea for showing a void is worth borrowing from the Little Major. With two Aces, plus a void in the lower-ranking of the remaining suits, the responder to 4NT bids Six Clubs. With two Aces and a void in the higher-ranking suit, he bids Six Diamonds. The special merit of this arrangement is that responder can sometimes indicate a void in his partner's suit—normally impossible to convey.

South	North
—	1 ♠
2 ◇	2 ♡
4 ♡	4NT
?	

South holds: ♠—   ♡ J 10 6 3   ◇ A J 8 6 2   ♣ A 7 5 4

South bids Six Diamonds, denoting two Aces and a void in spades. North can now bid a grand slam on:

♠ Q 10 8 6 3   ♡ A K Q 8 4   ◇ K Q   ♣ 10

TRUMP ASKING BIDS

The traditional responses to the 5NT grand slam force (asking for Seven when two top honours are held) are so wasteful of space that all other methods are an improvement. We suggest the following simple scheme:

Six Clubs	No top honour (A, K or Q)
Six Diamonds	One top honour
Six Hearts	Two top honours
Six Spades	Three top honours

The convention will now serve a player who holds, say, A Q x x x of the trump suit and needs to find partner with the King; or a player holding J x x x x who can bid Seven only if partner holds A K Q.

The 5NT grand slam force can be played alongside the Baron grand slam try. In this convention a bid of Six in the suit below the agreed trump suit asks partner to bid Seven if his trumps are good in relation to his previous bidding.

THE COMIC NO-TRUMP

It is advantageous, when not vulnerable, to play an overcall of 1NT as a two-way bid: either a normal 15-17, or a 'nonsense' containing a long suit. This is the Gardener No-trump Overcall, known on the Continent as the *sans-atout comique*. The partner of the overcaller easily discovers which type of hand is held.

| *South* | *West* | *North* | *East* |
| 1 ♣ | 1NT | Pass | ? |

East responds as follows:

Pass	When he would not try for game even if he knew partner held a genuine no-trump.
2 ♣	When opposite a genuine overcall he would entertain hopes of game. West then 'comes clean', bidding either his escape suit or, if genuine, 2NT or 3NT. (Two Clubs here has no relation to the opening One Club.)
2 ◇, 2 ♡, 2 ♠	When he has a long, self-supporting suit and would not try for game even over a genuine 1NT.

The Comic no-trump should not be regarded merely as a

bluff or controlled psychic. Its value is that it extends the
range of overcalls by enabling a defender to intervene on a
poor hand containing a long suit, without suggesting to partner that he has the values for a normal overcall. Thus it per-
forms the role of the weak jump overcall—not quite at the
same level but sufficiently high to pose problems for the
opposition. Meanwhile, the jump overcall itself is available
as a fairly strong bid on one-suited hands.

The overcall may also be used after both opponents have
bid:

South	*West*	*North*	*East*
1♣	Pass	1♢	1NT

East may hold a genuine no-trump or, at favourable vulnerability, something of this sort:

♠5   ♡KJ10874   ♢82   ♣10963

The opponents will probably know quite well what is
going on, but the overcall impedes the flow of constructive
bidding.

Note, in this last example, that if East had passed on the
first round the subsequent bid of 1NT would not be Comic
but 'Unusual', denoting length in the two unbid suits. The
Comic no-trump operates only when, on the surface, the bid
could be genuine.

The reader may be reflecting that, in response to the overcall of 1NT, Two Clubs appears to be ambiguous. Does it
ask whether the 1NT bid is genuine, or is it Stayman as proposed in Chapter 7? Players to whom both techniques appeal
may differentiate according to vulnerability. Not vulnerable,
Two Clubs asks, 'Are you Comic?' Vulnerable, it is a Stayman enquiry.

Countering the Comic no-trump. Against opponents who
have announced this weapon, it is a mistake to double in-
differently on all medium to strong hands.

South	*West*	*North*	*East*
1♢	1NT	?	

Here North only loses time and clarity by doubling the

intervention on a powerful hand. The double should show specifically 8 to 10 points. 2NT and 3NT should be natural and bids of Two in a new suit, normally limited, should be constructive.

WEAK CUE-BIDS

Since the dawn of time an immediate overcall in an opponent's suit has, for most players, signified a 'giant'. As defenders seldom reside in Brobdingnag, the bid is grossly underemployed.

It is sensible, therefore, to devise a more productive role. One possible use for the overcall is to denote a limited two-suiter, another to denote a distributional hand lacking the high cards for a take-out double. On grounds of frequency we recommend something in between, a method similar to the Michaels Cue-bid, popular in North America, but differing in some points of details.

Two Clubs over One Club, Two Diamonds over One Diamond. These overcalls, in second position only, are the equivalent of a sub-standard double containing, as a minimum, 5-4 in the majors. As in the Michaels Cue-bid, the point-count is from 6 to 10. This is a wide range, but tolerable between partners who have good tactical appreciation and whose morale will sustain an occasional calamity. At any vulnerability overcall One Diamond with Two Diamonds on each of the following. At favourable vulnerability you may even feel that you can spare a point or two.

(1) ♠ Q J 8 6 ♡ K 10 7 6 4 ♢ 3 ♣ K 8 4

(2) ♠ Q 9 7 4 2 ♡ A Q 10 6 3 ♢ 7 ♣ 4 2

(3) ♠ K J 10 6 ♡ A 8 7 6 4 2 ♢ — ♣ J 5 4

When partner holds a fit for either major he bids the full value of his hand. Other responses are limited and non-forcing.

Two Spades over One Spade. An overcall of Two Spades carries the auction quite high and the manoeuvre makes sense only on a pronounced two-suiter. As a minor two-suiter can be shown by an overcall of 2NT, a cue-bid of Two Spades should show hearts and one of the minors. These would be typical hands:

(1) ♠4 ♡KJ963 ♢A98653 ♣7

(2) ♠— ♡QJ853 ♢Q72 ♣KJ1086

After the Two Spade cue-bid, responder can ask for the second suit by bidding 2NT.

Two Hearts over One Heart. The overcall of Two Hearts has the character of a light double, with the important safety requirement of five spades. Bid Two Hearts over One Heart on any of the following:

(1) ♠Q9752 ♡4 ♢A962 ♣K87

(2) ♠J86542 ♡— ♢A85 ♣K974

(3) ♠K9863 ♡— ♢A107 ♣QJ852

A response of 2NT to this overcall is natural. On (1) and (2) the overcaller would pass 2NT; on (3) he would take out into Three Clubs.

The assurance of some support for both minors enables responder to get into the action more often than if the overcall denoted a two-suiter.

South	West	North	East
1♡	2♡	3♡	?

East holds: ♠54 ♡1063 ♢A108653 ♣J7

If West had overcalled with One Spade, or if the bid of Two Hearts might be based on spades and clubs only, East would be condemned to silence; but when West is marked with some support for the minors, East can bid Four Diamonds, inviting a sacrifice.

Some side benefits attach to these weak cue-bids. A player who has made a bid with a fixed upper limit is well placed afterwards to double co-operatively. For example, if you bid Two Clubs over One Club on a 'maximum' 10 points, you can double later without deceiving partner as to your defensive strength. Furthermore, the availability of the weak cue-bids removes the temptation to double for take-out on the proverbial tram-tickets, inviting reproach from a partner who takes unsuccessful action in consequence.

We are well aware that these manoeuvres on distributional hands are liable to assist the opponents if they gain the contract and are tigers at dummy play. Once the auction becomes competitive you may have to battle on up to a high level to prevent opponents from playing the hand with the advantage of special knowledge.

In fourth position. The weak cue-bid is not used now. The overcall in an opponent's suit reverts to its traditional role.

South	West	North	East
1 ◊	Pass	Pass	2 ◊

East must be allowed this means of introducing a powerfully distributed hand. It is unsatisfactory to double when a penalty pass by partner would be most unwelcome.

MODIFIED DRURY

At duplicate, as was noted at several points in the early chapters, small gains on the score-sheet bring good rewards in terms of match-points. This leads to pressure in favour of light openings in third or fourth hand. To throw in a combined 22 or 23 points may produce a poor score in a competitive field.

The Drury convention is designed to increase the safety of light openings by making it possible to stay at a low level when the responder has a fair hand. It operates only over a third- or fourth-hand opening of One Heart or One Spade. A bid of Two Clubs by the player who has passed is then conventional, asking opener to indicate whether his hand is sound or sub-minimum.

In the American form of the convention any rebid other than Two Diamonds proclaims a sound opening. When the rebid is Two Diamonds, responder assumes for the present that the opening was sub-minimum.

A defect in this procedure is that responder's second bid

will sometimes cross the intentions of the opening bidder.
For example:

West	*East*
♠ K J 9 7 6 4	♠ 5 2
♡ 5 3	♡ K 8 7
◇ A 10 8	◇ K J 4
♣ J 6	♣ A 10 5 3 2

West opens One Spade fourth in hand. When East makes
the Drury response of Two Clubs, West must bid Two Diamonds because he is sub-minimum. All would be well if East
held three spades and could bid Two Spades now, but in this
instance he bids 2NT and the hand is probably out of control.
Here Drury has failed to improve on the normal sequence
(assuming West opens) of 1♠—2♣—2♠—2NT or 1♠—
2♣—Pass.

The convention works better if the rebidding procedure is
reversed. When the opener is sub-minimum but has a strong
suit, let him sign off in his own suit. A rebid of Two Diamonds
suggests in principle a sound opening but may also be quite
weak on occasions when the opener's major is not rebiddable.

On the hand above, therefore, West rebids Two Spades,
closing shop. The sequence One Spade—Two Diamonds—
Two Hearts is also weak, showing a hand such as:

(1) ♠ A Q 8 6 3   ♡ K 10 5 2   ◇ 4   ♣ J 9 7

(2) ♠ K J 8 6 3   ♡ A J 9 6 4   ◇ 6 3   ♣ 4

The system of responses and rebids in Modified Drury is
based on the assumption that the opener, if sub-minimum,
has a five-card major. Of course, an opener who has no five-
suit may encounter a Two Club response, but on those
occasions he should have a sound rebid. Putting it another
way, if you open light with only a four-card major, you cannot rely on Drury to provide a safe landing.

It is possible to play Drury—many have attempted it—in
a free-and-easy form with no understanding beyond that set
out above. To obtain good results, however, it is necessary to
chart the meaning of various later sequences. We therefore
study the workings of Modified Drury under these headings:

1. The first response by a passed hand.
2. Opener's rebid.
3. Responder's second bid.
4. Some special sequences.

1. *The first response by a passed hand.* Do not bid a Drury Two Clubs on a hand that presents a natural response in a new suit. Use it only on hands of about 10 to 12 points, containing no biddable side suit and worth normally a response of 2NT or a double raise of opener's suit.

Over One Spade these are typical hands for a response of Two clubs:

(1) ♠ K J 8 6   ♡ Q 7   ♢ A 7 4 2   ♣ 10 6 4

Not playing Drury, you would have a somewhat unattractive raise to Three Spades.

(2) ♠ 6 4 2   ♡ K 5 2   ♢ A Q 6 2   ♣ K 7 5

This time Drury saves you from having to bid 2NT, with the familiar sequel of one or two down when partner has opened light.

(3) ♠ 10 2   ♡ A 9 4 3   ♢ A K 6   ♣ 7 6 5 4

Drury is welcome on this otherwise 'unbiddable' hand.

The convention may also be employed on strong supporting hands, worth a raise to game. See paragraph 4 below.

2. *Opener's rebid.* Over any response but Two Clubs, opener makes the same call as if not playing the convention. Over Two Clubs a simple rebid of opener's suit is weak.

(1) ♠ J 4   ♡ K 10 8 6 4 2   ♢ A J 7 3   ♣ 6

Open One Heart, rebid Two Hearts.

As we said earlier, Two Hearts following One Spade is also weak:

(2) ♠ J 9 7 6 4   ♡ A K 8 3   ♢ Q 2   ♣ 6 4

Open One Spade and over Two Clubs rebid Two Hearts, meaning *pas grande chose!*

A rebid of Two Diamonds is forcing and two-way: often a sound opening but consistent also with a weak opening. It follows that when opener with a good hand has bid Two Diamonds over Two Clubs, he must show his additional values clearly on the next round. Of course, you are not restricted to bidding Two Diamonds every time you hold a sound opening opposite a Drury response. Other rebids, such as 2NT, a jump in the original suit, or Three of a new suit, are all natural and take into account that the responder has shown fair values.

3. Responder's second bid. When opener rebids Two Diamonds, responder must still allow for the possibility of a weak opening. The following will be common sequences:

(1)

	South	North
	—	Pass
	1 ♠	2 ♣
	2 ◇	3 ♣

North holds a hand which would be worth a raise to Four over a sound opening.

(2)

	South	North
	—	Pass
	1 ♠	2 ♣
	2 ◇	2 ♡

North has precisely four hearts, otherwise he would have bid Two Hearts on the first round. (Responder does not employ the Drury convention when a satisfactory response in a new suit is available.)

(3)

	South	North
	—	Pass
	1 ♠	2 ♣
	2 ◇	2 ♠

North will be in the 10 to 11 range, with three spades, or the 9-10 range with four spades.

(4)

	South	North
	—	Pass
	1 ♠	2 ♣
	2 ◇	2NT

This is a slightly stronger sequence. North will have about 11-12 points—a normal 2NT response to an opening bid.

(5)	*South*	*North*
	—	Pass
	1 ♡	2 ♣
	2 ◇	2 ♠

Here North's bidding is natural, with five or six clubs and four spades. If he had spades only, not clubs, he would respond One Spade.

(6)	*South*	*North*
	—	Pass
	1 ♡	2 ♣
	2 ◇	3 ♣

Natural, with long clubs.

4. *Some special sequences.* The Two Club response provides an extra echelon of bids in some situations. Compare these two hands, both worth a raise to game opposite a sound opening of One Heart.

(1) ♠ 5 ♡ A 10 7 6 4 ◇ K 9 4 3 ♣ J 6 2

(2) ♠ K 4 ♡ A 9 8 5 2 ◇ A 7 6 ♣ 8 5 3

On (1), the distributional type, raise direct to Three Hearts. Partner knows you are allowing lee-way in case he is sub-minimum.

On (2), where you have a full quota of high cards as well as good trump support, begin with Two Clubs. Then over Two Diamonds bid Three Hearts.

A jump in a new suit is an additional resource for a strong passed hand. This has the normal Acol meaning—the values for a raise to Three, plus a side suit. If opener then makes a minimum rebid in his suit, that is a sign-off.

There remain two sequences in which responder may proceed to 2NT even though the opener may be weak. Take, first, the post-Drury 2NT:

(4)	*South*	*North*
	—	Pass
	1 ♠	2 ♣
	2 ♠	2NT

This sequence by responder almost guarantees that he is void of spades, with long clubs; a hand such as:

♠ — ♡ Q 10 6 ◇ A 9 5 3 ♣ K 10 8 6 4 2

Opener may now scramble for safety in clubs, or possibly in diamonds.

Finally, what of a direct response of 2NT? As one of the aims of Modified Drury is to avoid hoisting the auction to 2NT on a balanced 11 points, this response is definitely 'unusual'. So, an easy-to-remember suggestion is that a direct 2NT should signify both minors, a hand such as:

♠ 5 ♡ Q 7 ◇ K 10 8 3 2 ♣ A J 7 6 5

♠ J 9 ♡ — ◇ Q 10 6 4 3 ♣ K J 8 6 4 2

Over the direct 2NT, a take-out by opener into Three Clubs or Three Diamonds is not forcing. This particular variation, giving such an accurate account of the responding hand, will be particularly useful when the opener is genuine. Now, of course, he must jump to express good support for one of the minors, a bid of Three Clubs or Three Diamonds being a sign-off.

There is more to Modified Drury, obviously, than one would think from a short description. A player who masters all the sequences and employs them with good judgment is fully entitled to write M.D. after his name.

MAINLY ABOUT ASPRO

As opening bids of 1NT become more and more frequent in the tournament game, so the defence against them becomes more critical. As was remarked in Chapter 7, players are beginning to lose confidence in the double and are making more use of conventional overcalls.

Two simple conventions are known by the names of (among others) Landy and Ripstra. In *Landy* an overcall of Two

Clubs indicates a minimum of nine cards in the majors, divided 5-4. A typical hand would be:

♠ K J 8 6 4   ♡ A Q 8 6   ◇ 5 4   ♣ K 3

Partner's responses are natural. With support for a major he makes a value bid. The only forcing response is Three Clubs.

In the *Ripstra* convention both Two Clubs and Two Diamonds are conventional. They denote tolerance for the named minor suit as well as support for both majors. The following is a typical Ripstra overcall of Two Diamonds:

♠ K 1 0 8 3   ♡ K 9 7 5 2   ◇ A Q 4   ♣ 4

Players using Ripstra have a good chance of landing on their feet, but hands suitable for the convention are infrequent as there must be preparedness for three suits, including both majors. Thus too many competitive opportunities are missed.

A third method mentioned earlier was *Astro*, in which Two Diamonds indicates spades and another suit, Two Clubs indicates hearts and a minor suit. The convention has the advantage that it can be used on most two-suited and semibalanced hands.

We recommend a variation known known as *Aspro*, which follows out the basic idea of Astro but differs in some important respects. It is used both in second and fourth position. An overcall of Two Clubs shows hearts and another suit, Two Diamonds shows spades and a minor suit. The normal minimum is about 10 high-card points. Any of the following would be suitable for an Aspro overcall:

(1)   ♠ 1 0 6   ♡ A K J 8 3   ◇ K J 9 6 4   ♣ 4

(2)   ♠ K 7 3   ♡ A Q 8 6 3   ◇ 4   ♣ K Q 1 0 7

(3)   ♠ K J 1 0 3   ♡ 8 2   ◇ A K 1 0 8 4   ♣ K 9

(4)   ♠ A Q 1 0 3   ♡ 8 7   ◇ 6   ♣ A J 9 7 4 2

On (1) and (2) overcall with Two Clubs, on (3) and (4) with Two Diamonds. Later developments with these hands are explained on the next page.

DEVELOPMENTS AFTER AN ASPRO OVERCALL

Say that the bidding has begun:

South	West	North	East
1NT	2♣	Pass	?

Responses by East have the following significance:

Pass   Weak hand with at least five clubs.

2♠   Limited hand with long spades.

2NT   Natural.

2♡   At least three hearts (partner's suit), limited values.

3♡, 4♡   Stronger support for hearts. Responder with a fit for the major can raise to about the same level as he would raise an opening bid.

2♢   A relay, indicating a limited hand with not more than a doubleton in the anchor suit (hearts). Diamonds may be the long suit and will not be less than a doubleton. The Aspro bidder, over the relay, may bid Two Hearts with a five-card suit, or pass Two Diamonds, or bid his second suit.

3♣   This raise of the artificial suit is the only force.

Responses to an overcall of Two Diamonds follow the same scheme, the relay now being Two Hearts.

To illustrate further, we return to hands (1) to (4) above. In each case South has opened 1NT and West has made an Aspro overcall. This was the first hand:

(1)   ♠ 10 6   ♡ A K J 8 3   ♢ K J 9 8 4   ♣ 4

Having overcalled with Two Clubs, West will pass a relay response of Two Diamonds or a minimum response of Two Hearts, the anchor suit.

(2)   ♠ K 7 3   ♡ A Q 8 6 3   ♢ 4   ♣ K Q 10 7

This time, with a five-card anchor suit, West will bid Two

Hearts over a relay response of Two Diamonds. If responder
has a singleton heart he may now introduce spades on a
moderate suit (which on this occasion would suit West well
enough) or bid 2NT, asking West to name his minor suit.

(3) ♠ K J 10 3   ♡ 8 2   ◇ A K 10 8 4   ♣ K 9

West overcalls with Two Diamonds and East bids a relay
Two Hearts. Now West bids Three Diamonds, for East would
have bid Two Spades if he held as many as three cards in the
suit. As this sequence takes the bidding uncomfortably high,
it follows that a defender who has no five-card major should
not embark on Aspro unless he is strong.

(4) ♠ A Q 10 3   ♡ 8 7   ◇ 6   ♣ A J 9 7 4 2

Again West overcalls with Two Diamonds. If he receives a
response of Two Spades it will be wise to remove to Three
Clubs, for the hand might be unplayable in a 4-2 fit. If
partner in fact holds four spades and is short in clubs he will
revert to spades.

Aspro on a major two-suiter. The general rule on a major
two-suiter is to overcall with Two Clubs.

(1) ♠ A Q 9 7   ♡ K Q 5 3 2   ◇ 4 2   ♣ K 5

Bid Two Clubs over 1NT. If partner shows support for
hearts, you are satisfied. Over a relay response of Two Diamonds continue with Two Spades, not Two Hearts (where
partner is known to be short). Lacking tolerance for either
major, partner can convert to 2NT.

(2) ♠ K Q 5 3 2   ♡ A Q 9 7   ◇ 4 2   ♣ K 5

Again overcall with Two Clubs. Continue with Two
Spades over Two Diamonds and also over Two Hearts. (In the
latter case you show your distribution precisely.) Bid the same
way with 5-5 in the majors.

Expressing a three-suiter. In some sequences the Aspro
bidder can convey that he has a three-suiter.

(1)   *South*   *West*   *North*   *East*
          1NT   2 ◇   Pass   2 ♡
          Pass   ?

West holds: ♠ A 10 9 6   ♡ —   ◇ Q J 9 5   ♣ A Q 7 4 2

A bid of 2NT by West now must mean length in both minors, for his normal action, if not intending to bid Two Spades, would be to name his second suit.

(2)   *South*   *West*   *North*   *East*
          1NT   2 ♣   Pass   2 ◇
          Pass   2NT

West holds: ♠ 4   ♡ A Q 8 4   ◇ K J 9 3   ♣ K 10 7 4

As East is short in hearts there must be a landing-place in one of the minors. (With this particular distribution it is fairly safe for West to ignore the normal Aspro rule that nine cards should be held in two suits.)

Aspro on stronger hands. The upper limit for an Aspro overcall may be set at about 16 points.

♠ A Q 10 6 3   ♡ K 8   ◇ 5 4   ♣ A Q J 4

Prefer an Aspro overcall to a double. If partner, with long diamonds, passes the overcall, it will not necessarily be a bad spot. If he bids Two Spades you may venture Three Spades.

Some discretion is needed on pronounced two-suiters because of the possibility that partner may pass the overcall.

♠ A J 10 4 2   ♡ —   ◇ K 6 3   ♣ A K J 8 5

Here it is safe to overcall with Two Diamonds because it is unlikely that partner will be long enough in diamonds to pass; also, someone is likely to bid hearts.

♠ A J 7 4 2   ♡ K 6   ◇ —   ♣ A Q J 8 7 6

Now Two Diamonds would be an error as partner might well pass it. Best is to overcall 2NT, denoting a non-Aspro combination: that is to say, not spades-and-diamonds or hearts-and-clubs.

It is possible to devise conventional meanings for overcalls at the Three level, but the advantage, as compared with using

these bids in a natural sense, is doubtful. Over 1NT, bid
Three of a suit with a hand such as:

♠ A 3   ♡ 5   ◇ 7 4 2   ♣ A Q J 9 8 6 3

Competitive manoeuvres. If an Aspro overcall is doubled,
a pass by fourth hand signifies willingness to play.

South	West	North	East
1NT	2♣	Double	?

A pass by East promises a minimum of four cards in the
suit doubled; with fewer, he must redouble for rescue or
remove to another suit. In all Aspro sequences a redouble is
a distress signal.

Double by a passed hand. The suggestion made on page
83 that a double by a passed hand should denote either a
major or a minor two-suiter fits in very well with the Aspro
method. It will mean in effect that after an Aspro overcall
the responder will often know at once the two suits held by
his partner.

SUMMARY OF CONVENTIONS

The following are the main features of the conventions
described in this chapter:

Slam conventions. Use the CRO variation of Roman Blackwood (Colour, Rank, Odd). To ask for Kings, bid the next-
ranking suit when not a possible trump suit. Use also the
void-showing responses to 4NT: Six Diamonds to show two
Aces and a void in the higher-ranking of the remaining suits,
Six Clubs to show two Aces and a void in the lower suit.

Over a Trump Asking Bid of 5NT bid Six Clubs with no
top honour, Six Diamonds with one, and so on.

The Comic no-trump. When not vulnerable, 1NT over an
opponent's opening bid may be either 15 to 17 points or a
'nonsense'. In response to the overcall, Two Clubs asks for
clarification. When opponents are using the Comic no-trump,
double the overcall only on 8-10 points.

Modified Drury. In response to partner's third- or fourth-hand opening bid of One Heart or One Spade, bid Two Clubs to test whether he is up to strength (but only when no natural response in a new suit is available).

When you have opened light in third or fourth position and partner has responded Two Clubs, rebid your suit (or follow One Spade with Two Hearts) to show a weak opening. With a sound opening bid Two Diamonds or make any natural rebid at a higher level. Also bid Two Diamonds with a weak opening and a non-rebiddable major.

Weak cue-bids. In second position, cue-bid the opponent's minor suit to show 5-4 in the majors. Bid Two Hearts over One Heart with five spades and tolerance for both minors. Bid Two Spades over One Spade with five hearts and a five-card minor.

Aspro. Over an opponent's 1NT opening, in either second or fourth position bid Two Diamonds with spades and a minor suit, Two Clubs with hearts and any other suit. When responding to Aspro, either show values in the anchor suit, or bid a long suit of your own, or pass with length in the suit of the overcall, or make a relay bid in the next-ranking suit. To force, raise the Aspro bid.

When your partner's Aspro bid has been doubled, pass only with four cards or more in the suit doubled. With fewer, bid another suit or redouble.

SHEDDING THE LOAD

Tournament Acol, as set out in the last four chapters, will no doubt strike some readers as a complicated system, perhaps unduly so. It is worth remembering that these things are relative: if one were starting from scratch the present body of conventions, familiar to all tournament players, would seem a fearsome collection. It is not difficult to build slowly on what one already knows.

Many of the conventions we have described are optional and not interdependent. We do not suggest that the whole apparatus should be employed in every form of contest, even if the rules allow it. There is a difference between understandings in constructive bidding, which should be explained when they occur but do not put opponents at a disadvantage, and a competitive manoeuvre like Aspro, which is difficult to counter without prior arrangement. In a club event, or an open pairs at a Congress, play simply the conventions that everyone knows. In team events, or a pairs where all the players are experienced, you will need a more elaborate system.

11

VISIONS OF THE FUTURE

How old is contract bridge? Only about forty years. For a game with an intricate and elaborate technique, that is nothing. It would be rash to assume that no great discoveries remain to be made.

Of course, there may be different views about the desirability of radical change. There was a time, in the mid-fifties, when the use of bids as ciphers unrelated to the suit named might have been barred by the world authorities. However, the necessary stand was not taken and the point of no return has surely been passed. Artificial bids are still held in partial check, but their opponents lack any clear rallying point. It is at least possible that within twenty years bidding will be conducted in a language that would be unrecognisable today.

Not many tournament players are willing to be left behind when changes are in the wind, so in this chapter we examine the most promising.

THE RELAY PRINCIPLE

When reading the section on Modified Drury you may have been struck by the fact that the artificial Two Club response, though designed primarily to protect weak openings, at the same time extended the range of bids open to the responding hand. Thus One Spade—Three Spades meant one thing, One Spade—Two Clubs—Two Diamonds—Three Spades another. A direct response of 2NT to an opening bid conveyed a different meaning from 2NT reached by way of Drury.

The fact is that the use of artificial responses at a low level almost doubles the number of ways in which responder can express his hand. The Gladiator response of Two Clubs over INT, described on page 143, is one bid that exploits this advantage. Some Continental systems are largely based on it. In the Swedish Efos method, and also in the Roman system, a response in the next suit, such as One Heart over One Diamond, has no relation to the suit named. Space is saved and a responder who, for example, holds a spade suit may bid a direct One Spade, or a direct Two Spades, or Two Spades following the artificial response. The effect of this style, in Swift's phrase, is to make two (or more) ears of corn grow where one grew before.

THE TRANSFER PRINCIPLE

Transfers provide another way of increasing the productivity of bids. The Flint convention (Three Diamonds over 2NT) is a familiar example. Transfer bids at a lower level may give the responder even more room for manoeuvre. Say that the bidding begins:

South	North
1NT	2 ♡ (transfer)
2 ♠	

Now North may pass or raise to Three Spades or bid 2NT or 3NT or make a trial bid such as Three Clubs. Clearly the range of expression is superior to anything that can be contrived within the same space by non-conventional methods.

In some Continental systems transfer bids are freely used after suit openings as well as after no-trump openings. In the Little Major (of which we shall be giving an outline later in this chapter), some opening bids are transfers in effect. Used in conjunction with a negative response, this method provides responder with numerous ways of developing his hand. For example, after an opening One Club, denoting hearts, the following possibilities exist for a responder who has moderate support:

1 ♣—1 ◇—1 ♡—Pass	With a worthless or near-worthless hand responder bids the negative One Diamond and may pass opener's rebid of One Heart, which itself is limited.
1 ♣—1 ♡	The response shows four trumps and 3 to 7 points.
1 ♣—1 ◇—1 ♡—2 ♡	This sequence shows three trumps, a ruffing value, and 6 to 8 points.
1 ♣—2 ♡	Equal to a maximum Acol raise to Two Hearts.

At Acol the responder might pass on the first hand; the others would all be expressed by the same single raise.

In the Little Major only the opening One Club and One Diamond bids are transfers, but it won't be long before someone builds up a complete system based on the same idea. Long vistas immediately come into view!

We turn now to a concept which lies at the heart, not only of relays and transfer bids, but also of such homely manoeuvres as simple Blackwood. This is the 'Interrogator' concept.

THE INTERROGATOR

Many possible developments turn on the relationship between two players engaged in a constructive sequence. It is usual to think of bidding as an exchange in which each player gives a picture of his holding, but it is equally possible for one player to do all the asking and his partner all the telling. Thus in the French 'relay' system the responder, saying nothing about his own hand until the finish, may make a series of bids which ask the opener to give a detailed account of his strength and distribution.

This 'Interrogator' method may well be the style of the future, especially when the opening bid falls within fairly narrow limits. Here is an imaginary sequence, not related to any existing system:

South	North
1 ♠ [1]	1NT [2]
2 ◇ [3]	2 ♡ [4]
3 ♣ [5]	3 ◇ [6]
3NT [7]	4 ♣ [8]
4 ♡ [9]	6NT [10]
Pass	

1. 'I am in the 12-17 range with a five-card suit.'
2. 'Tell me your range.'
3. 'I am 14-15.' (Two Clubs would show 12-13.)
4. 'Tell me whether you have another four-card suit.'
5. 'Yes, clubs.' (2NT would deny.)
6. 'How many Aces have you?'
7. 'Two.' (On the step principle)
8. 'How many Kings?'
9. 'One.'
10. 'I have heard all I want.'

A sentiment with which the reader may agree!

LIGHT OPENINGS

It is unlikely that the traditional standards for opening bids will survive much longer. The logical basis, in so far as there is any, for the present standard is that if both players hold less than 12 points it is unlikely there will be a game in the two hands. That ignores the competitive side of bidding. The plain fact is that it is usually more difficult to bid accurately against an opening bid than when given a free run. If it is sound to overcall at the One level on A Q J x x, then it must equally be good tactics to open so long as it can be organized with reasonable safety and without loss of efficiency in constructive bidding. As techniques improve, more troops will be available to serve on the defensive front.

There have already been experiments with very weak openings, such as the ultra-weak no-trump and the attractively named LOBs (Light Opening Bids) proposed by two young players several years ago. In time, defensive openings at the One level may be routine.

NEGATIVE DOUBLES

The competitive doubles and unassuming cue-bids described in Chapter 7 represent one form of progress. There will surely be more changes of this sort. One good idea that has been around for some time is the negative double. The bidding goes:

South	West	North	East
—	—	1 ◇	1 ♠

South holds: ♠ 9 4 2   ♡ K 8 7 3   ◇ Q 7   ♣ A 8 6 4

This is a familiar dilemma, to which there is no good answer unless negative doubles are used. Then South doubles One Spade, indicating a moderate degree of honour strength without reference to his holding in spades.

As it is rarely good tactics to double for penalties at the One level, this is undoubtedly a theoretical improvement. It may be that rubber-bridge players will never abandon the opportunity to wield the axe, but tournament players, we believe, will eventually adopt negative doubles at low levels. Some players extend the negative quality of the double up to the Three and even Four level. That, we are bound to say, is a concession we would not readily make to our best friends.

ADVANCES IN PLAY

There is certainly scope for innovation in the mechanics of signalling. A player who, discarding on an enemy suit, lets go three or four useless cards has opportunities to play many a tune for which no score has so far been written.

However, the most important development may lie in the mental attitude of a player who makes a signal. We suggest in the next chapter that a defender should form his own estimate of what his partner will want to know and should signal in a way that will depend on the logic of the situation as viewed by the defending side. One advantage is that signals made on that basis will not be easy for the declarer to 'unscramble'.

THE LITTLE MAJOR

We devote the rest of this chapter to an outline of the Little Major, partly because of the general interest in it and partly because it represents the first attempt to cut loose from all preconceptions about bidding and devise a method that takes the maximum advantage of bidding space. It is worth remarking that, historically, the system was invented as an Awful Warning of what might happen if every country playing in international championships were to arrive with its own wholly artificial system. However, the original motive was soon forgotten, for the point of the protest had already been overtaken by events and the project was found in itself to be extremely interesting.

The first somewhat artless notion was that opening bids of One Heart and One Spade should be purely obstructive, signifying a shortage in the suit and only 5 to 9 points. That is how the system first acquired the title of the Little Major. Meanwhile, One Club denoted hearts and One Diamond spades, 1NT serving for minor-suit hands. It soon became apparent that the openings of One Heart and One Spade, as inhibiting manoeuvres, were less effective than one might have imagined, while the use of two such important bids in a purely defensive role created too many problems in constructive bidding. This is the present scheme:

THE MAIN OPENING SEQUENCES

1♣	In principle, a heart suit. To this, One Diamond is a negative response but may also be the first move on a big hand.
1◇	Either a spade suit or a 16-19 no-trump. One Heart is a negative response but may also be the first move on a big hand.
1♡	Used on most hands from 20 points upwards and on all near-game hands. The bid is also available as a controlled psychic on weak hands in the 2 to 5 range.

1 ♠   Limited opening, about 12 to 15, with values in both minors, usually 5-4 or better.

1NT   Normal no-trump type, 13 to 15 throughout.

2 ♣, 2 ♦   Limited opening, about 12 to 15, with a fair minor suit.

These openings account for 95% of all hands. It will be observed that the One Club and One Diamond openings enable hands containing a major to be opened at a lower level than in standard systems, and the use of an artificial response greatly increases the number of ways in which the bidding can be developed. Meanwhile, hands containing length in the minors only, which are at a disadvantage in a competitive auction, are opened with the mildly pre-emptive bids of One Spade, Two Clubs and Two Diamonds.

Continuing the schedule:

2 ♡, 2 ♠   Strong major-minor two-suiter.

2NT   Equal to a weak Three bid in a minor; also available on strong minor two-suiters.

3 ♣, 3 ♦   Good suit, main values in the minors.

3 ♡, 3 ♠
Texas 4 ♣
and 4 ♦   } All as Acol.
4 ♡, 4 ♠

3NT   Solid minor, as Acol.

We now examine some of the main sequences in more detail.

OPENING ONE CLUB OR ONE DIAMOND

Almost all hands containing a four-card major are opened with 1 ♣ or 1 ♦ unless they qualify for 1 ♡, 2 ♡ or 2 ♠, or are suitable for 1NT. Sometimes it is necessary to bid (indirectly) a three-card major—usually on hands in the 16 to 19 range which are too strong for the limited openings 1 ♠, 2 ♣ or 2 ♦.

Open 1 ♣ on any of the following:

♠ 3   ♡ A 10 7 5   ◇ K Q 10 6 5 4   ♣ K 7

♠ K J 9 2   ♡ A Q 8 3   ◇ 10   ♣ K 10 4 3

♠ 6   ♡ A 10 4   ◇ K Q J 9   ♣ A K 7 6 4

♠ A K 2   ♡ 10 9 6 2   ◇ 9   ♣ A 8 7 5 4

Open 1 ◇ on:

♠ J 9 5 4   ♡ 8 3   ◇ A 6   ♣ A K 10 7 6

♠ K J 4   ♡ 2   ◇ A Q J 8 6 3   ♣ A Q 9

♠ K J 7 4 3   ♡ A K 9 8 6   ◇ 6   ♣ K 4

♠ K 10   ♡ A Q 3   ◇ K J 8 2   ♣ K Q 7 5

The One Diamond opening, it will be remembered may also show a 16-19 no-trump. The last hand is an example.

RESPONSES TO ONE CLUB AND ONE DIAMOND

Responder assumes, at the outset, that 1 ♣ stands for an opening One Heart, 1 ◇ for One Spade. Thus, over 1 ♣, any response in hearts is a value bid, showing support. Other responding hands fall into one of the following categories:

(a) *Negative, less than about 9 points*

With a weak hand responder first gives the negative answer, then passes or makes a minimum bid on the next round. Thus a sequence such as 1 ◇—1 ♡—1 ♠—2 ◇ indicates a limited hand with long diamonds.

(b) *Semi-positive, from about 9 points upwards*

A response of 1 ♠ (over 1 ♣) may be no more than a good 8 points, and a response of 2 ♣ has about the same minimum as Acol. These are both 'semi-positive' responses, forcing as far as Two of the opener's suit.

A response of 1NT is also classified as semi-positive and may be made on various types—balanced, containing a red suit, or containing support for partner. It is forcing for one round.

Over 1NT the opener, except on certain well-defined types,

rebids Two Clubs. Responder now has several ways of denoting a medium hand:

(1) 1♣—1NT—2♣—2◇   Medium, with diamond suit.

(2) 1♣—1NT—2♣—2♡   Medium, with three hearts.

(3) 1♣—1NT—2♣—2NT Medium, balanced.

A simpler scheme in which 1NT is a natural balanced 9 to 11, not forcing, is also quite playable.

(c) *Positive, from about 11 points upwards*

Since a medium hand with hearts or diamonds can be expressed by way of the forcing 1NT, an immediate 2◇ or 2♡ over an opening 1◇ is somewhat stronger. It promises a further bid unless opener rebids 2NT, which is minimum.

(d) *No-trump hands*

Balanced hands are expressed as follows: a negative, followed by 1NT, shows 7-9, 1NT followed by 2NT shows 10-11, an immediate 2NT 12-13, an immediate 3NT 14-15, 3NT after a negative 16-17, 3NT after the forcing 1NT 18-19.

(e) *Immediate forces*

An immediate jump in a new suit, 1♣—2♠ or 1♣—3♣, promises a powerful suit and game-going values.

(f) *Delayed forces*

On most strong hands responder first gives a negative, then jumps on the second round. 1◇—1♡—1♠—3♠ is a force based on trump support, 1◇—1♡—1♠—2NT asks opener to bid his four-card suits upwards, 1◇—1♡—1♠—3♣ shows clubs, but the strength of the suit is limited by the failure to force on the first round.

REBIDS BY THE ONE CLUB OR ONE DIAMOND OPENER

(a) *Over a negative response*

With a moderate hand the opener always rebids his nominated suit at minimum level.

♠2 ♡A J 8 6 ◇K Q 10 8 4 2 ♣Q 7

After 1♣—1◇ the rebid is 1♡. Then a later bid of diamonds will express the type.

♠K J 9 3 2 ♡A Q 8 7 4 ◇9 ♣J 2

Open 1◇ and, over 1♡, rebid 1♠.

A new suit over a negative, known as a 'low reverse', always means a fair hand.

♠A J 5 4 ♡5 ◇K Q 10 8 6 4 ♣A 7

Open 1◇, rebid 2◇.

♠K Q 9 2 ♡A K J 7 ◇10 ♣A 10 9 2

Open 1♣, rebid 1♠.

♠K J 10 6 3 ♡A Q J 8 ◇A 10 ♣4 2

Open 1◇, rebid 2♡.

With a powerful one-suited hand the opener may jump in the nominated suit. With a good hand containing a strong minor suit he may jump in the minor:

♠K 2 ♡A Q 6 2 ◇7 ♣A K J 8 5 3

Open 1♣, rebid 3♣, not forcing.

(b) *Over a positive response*

Over a positive or semi-positive response the opener for the most part develops his hand naturally. Bidding a second suit no longer denotes strength. Rebids in no-trumps are natural, taking into account the minimum strength shown by responder.

(c) *Over the forcing 1NT*

After 1◇—1NT, a bid of 2♠ means a limited hand with long spades. 2◇ would be a 'correction' type—weak opening with long diamonds—and 2♡ would mean long clubs. 2NT would be a strong no-trump. Bids at the Three level are analagous to jump rebids over a negative. On all other hands the opener bids a relay Two Clubs.

(d) *Specialised sequences denoting a three-suiter*

No-trump hands of 20 or more are opened with 1 ♡. Thus 1 ♣—1 ◇—2NT is available to denote a strong three-suiter with short spades, 1 ◇—1 ♡—2NT a three-suiter with short hearts.

(e) *Strong no-trump sequences*

The sequence 1 ♣—1 ◇—1NT denotes a 16-19 balanced hand containing a heart suit worth mentioning.

The sequence 1 ◇—1 ♡—1NT denotes a 16-19 no-trump which may or may not contain some length in spades and may, if balanced, contain a biddable heart suit. The responses after 1 ♣—1 ◇—1NT and 1 ◇—1 ♡—1NT are on the same lines as over the opening 1NT, described below (Two Clubs gladiator and Two Diamonds general enquiry).

In general, a rebid of no-trumps by a player who has opened 1 ◇ means that the opening was of the no-trump type. The exception is when 2NT is bid over a positive at the Two level: 1 ◇—2 ♣—2NT shows a minimum opening containing a spade suit.

Taking the remaining opening bids in a rough order of frequency, we look next at the opening 1NT. The scheme is adaptable to any system and to any range of no-trump opening.

OPENING 1NT, 13 TO 15

The opening 1NT necessarily covers many hands with a five-card minor suit not good enough for an opening 2 ♣ or 2 ◇. When the strength is right, it may also be made on many hands with biddable hearts or spades.

The system of responses is based on a combination of Two Clubs (gladiator) and 2 ◇ (general enquiry). First, we summarise the non-conventional replies:

Responses to 1NT

2 ♡, 2 ♠   Natural, weak.

2NT   Natural, 10-11.

3 ♣   A hand containing one or both minors, where a minor-suit contract may be preferable to 3NT, e.g.

♠ A J   ♡ 7   ◇ K 10 8 6 4   ♣ Q J 9 8 2

♠ 9   ♡ Q 8 3   ◇ K Q 10 9 6 3   ♣ A J 7

The opener rebids 3NT with both majors held, 3 ♡ or 3 ♠ with a double guard in that suit, otherwise 3 ◇.

3 ◇   Medium major two-suiter, e.g.

♠ K 9 6 3 2   ♡ Q J 9 5 3   ◇ 10   ♣ A 4

This response calls for a jump to game if opener has fair support for either suit.

3 ♡, 3 ♠   Long suit, invitational.

4 ♣, 4 ◇   Texas.

Response of 2 ♣ (gladiator)

The opener always rebids 2 ◇. Responder may pass this with a weak diamond hand. Continuations of 2 ♡, 2 ♠, 3 ♣ and 3 ◇ are constructive, not forcing. 2NT asks for suits upwards. 3 ♡ and 3 ♠ are forcing, and 3NT a slam suggestion, 18-19. 2NT by a passed hand shows 11-12.

Response of 2◇ (general enquiry)

This is a sort of 'constructive Stayman'. Opener shows a four-card major, bids 2NT, or Three of a minor with a fair suit and above-minimum hand. The bidding may stop in 2NT but not elsewhere below game.

Opening Two Clubs and Two Diamonds

These bids indicate a limited hand with a fair suit and normally no four-card major. Responses of 2NT and 3NT are natural. A single raise is constructive, a double raise pre-emptive. Suit responses are forcing for one round.

OPENING ONE SPADE

In principle a limited hand with length in both minors, usually 5-4 or better, such as:

♠5   ♡K86   ◇QJ972   ♣AK93

♠J5   ♡2   ◇AQ763   ♣KJ1054

The main conventional responses are 1NT and 2◇. We look at the other responses first.

Responses to 1♠

Pass   Correct on a moderate hand with long spades and no minor-suit length.

2♣   Limited, with support for clubs but not diamonds.

2♡, 2♠   Long suit, limited strength.

2NT   Playable at the Three level in either minor e.g.

♠K1082   ♡104   ◇Q1073   ♣J64

3NT   Similar to 2NT, with stronger distribution.

3♣, 3◇   Limited, with length in the suit.

♠96   ♡A943   ◇K10652   ♣72
Respond 3◇.

♠Q8643   ♡73   ◇K9   ♣QJ86
Respond 3♣.

Response of 1NT

For the moment this asks opener to name his long minor (or to bid 2◇ with 5-5). It is the first move when responder proposes to settle in partner's better suit at the Two level, or to convert Two Clubs to Two Diamonds, or to make a game try after hearing partner's minor. After 1♠—1NT—2◇, 2♡ or 2♠ are forcing for one round, 2NT and 3NT are natural.

Response of 2◇

This is the bid on most strong hands when responder needs time to develop and is more concerned with partner's major than minor holdings. The opener's first rebid describes his holding in the majors. With a major-suit 'bolster' (x x x or

Q x), he bids Two of the suit. Lacking a bolster, he bids 2NT or shows the long minor in a 6-4 hand. The response of 2 ◇ is forcing to game except that the bidding may be dropped in 4 ♣ or 4 ◇.

OPENING ONE HEART

Most hands of 20 points upwards, and all that would qualify for a Two bid at Acol, are opened 1 ♡. Responses to this opening are on the step principle. One Spade is weak, 1NT moderate, Two Clubs shows an Ace and a King, Two Diamonds two Aces or an Ace and two Kings. Two Hearts and Two Spades are natural and limited. After 1 ♡—1 ♠ the bidding may die at 2NT or at Three of a suit that is not a new suit.

In championship play (if not in domestic events) the opening 1 ♡ is available as a controlled psychic on hands in the 2 to 5 range. When responder is strong and suspects the weak opening he is not obliged to make the conventional responses. If very strong he may bid 3 ♡ or 3 ♠, invitational, or 2NT, forcing. A pass by the opener on the second round in all sequences denotes the psychic opening.

OPENING TWO HEARTS AND TWO SPADES

When an opening 1 ♣ or 1 ◇ is followed by the bid of a minor suit over a negative response, the minor suit is always at least as long as the major, and generally longer. Thus a different sequence is needed on strong major-minor two-suiters. The usual standards for an opening 2 ♡ or 2 ♠ are: 5-4-3-1 17 to 19, 5-5-2-1 16 to 19, somewhat less with a good 6-5. The sequence is not used on 5-4-2-2.

♠ K 10   ♡ A Q 9 4 2   ◇ A J 8 6   ♣ A 4

Open 1 ♣ and rebid 1 ♡ or 1NT.

♠ K 8 7 6 4   ♡ 10   ◇ A K J 10 2   ♣ A Q

The spades are too weak for 2 ♠. Open 1 ◇ and rebid 2 ◇ over a negative.

These are typical Two bids:

♠8   ♥AQJ65   ♦KQ108   ♣AJ4

♠AK1062   ♥10   ♦AKJ102   ♣A8

♠4   ♥AKJ832   ♦KQJ83   ♣5

The full pattern of responses and rebids is somewhat complicated. A playable method is to treat all responses below game, except for 2NT, as limited and non-forcing. The main conventional response is 2NT, asking the opener to describe his distribution according to the following schedule:

Rebids over 2NT (whether the opening was Two Hearts or Two Spades)

3♣ or 3♦	A five-card suit.
3♠	Four diamonds and three cards in the other major.
3♥	Four clubs and three cards in the other major.
3NT	A singleton in the other major, 4-3 or possibly 4-4 in the minors.

A return to partner's major at the Three level is not forcing.

OPENING 2NT

2NT is a two-way bid: usually a weak pre-empt in a minor, but occasionally a strong minor two-suiter.

Responder at first assumes 2NT to be equal to an opening 3♣ or 3♦ at Acol. When not intending to try for game if partner's suit is clubs, he takes out into Three Clubs. With possibilities for game in clubs but not in diamonds, he takes out into Three Diamonds. Opener will pass this if his suit is diamonds.

The opening 2NT is also available on a strong two-suiter such as:

♠A   ♥3   ♦AK865   ♣KQ10732

The type is indicated by any rebid inconsistent with the weak opening. If opponents are bidding, a double will usually be best.

Responses and rebids are natural, on the basis that the opener is not expected to hold more than a doubleton in either major.

OPENING THREE CLUBS AND THREE DIAMONDS

These bids serve for quite good hands containing a strong minor suit and little support for either major, such as:

♠5 ♡J6 ◇AQ4 ♣AKJ7643

INTERVENTION

We have not paused, in the course of this review, to study ways of dealing with intervention. Negative doubles are essential, but that is not the end of it. As we said at the beginning, our purpose is not to present a playable entity—just an impression of a futuristic system in the developing stage.

PART FOUR

Team-work

12

PLOTTING THE DEFENCE

This chapter deals first with special leads (Roman and MUD), secondly with signals and echoes.

SPECIAL LEADS

(a) *Roman*

Instead of the traditional top of a sequence, the second highest card is led from an honour combination—the Queen from K Q, Jack from Q J, and so on, down to the 9 from 10 9. From an interior sequence the principle of second highest still holds good: the Queen from A Q J, the Jack from K J 10, the 10 from K 10 9.

This method has demonstrable advantages over the traditional system. One clear gain is that the lead of the King is no longer ambiguous: it means A K x, not K Q. (Many players seek to resolve that ambiguity by leading Ace from A K x, but this creates another, though possibly minor, problem: a player who wants to lead the Ace from a suit such as A x x x x must take into account that partner may place him with A K.)

A second advantage arises when the Queen, Jack or 10 is led from an interior sequence. Here are two situations:

(1)   Q 6 5

             J led   A 8 4 3

Dummy plays low after the lead of the Jack and East, if defending against a high suit contract and playing normal leads, might be uncertain whether to put on the Ace. Playing Roman leads, East would know that partner held K J 10, for the lead from J 10 9 x x would be the 10.

(2)   K 7 4
                10 9 8 3   A 6 5
                          Q J 2

If West makes the traditional lead of the 10 against a no-trump contract, dummy will play low and South will win with the Jack. Now East cannot tell whether the lead was from Q 10 9 or 10 9. On the Roman lead of the 9 South would be marked with Q J.

Roman leads are normally played on the first trick only, though it is possible to follow the same principle throughout the play. They are not, as a matter of practice, employed when leading partner's suit.

(b) *Middle, up, down*

One of the oldest controversies concerns the best practice when leading from three spot cards, such as 8 6 3. The drawback—against a suit contract, particularly—of the old-fashioned top-of-nothing lead is that partner often cannot distinguish, even after the second card has been played, between a trebleton and a doubleton. Because of that difficulty some players prefer to lead the bottom card from three, while others follow the convention known as MUD (from the initials Middle, Up, Down). From 8 6 3 they lead the 6 and follow with the 8.

It is unnecessary, in matters of this sort, to pledge oneself to any fixed method, for the most helpful play depends very much on the individual situation. It is right to agree that the 6 followed by the eight should signify three cards (when it is clear that the 6 is not fourth best), but wrong to say in advance that you will always lead the middle card from three. The rank of the cards is one factor to consider: from 9 7 5 the 7 may commend itself, for it will not give partner the idea that you have led from an honour combination; but the 3 from 9 3 2 may well be misconstrued.

There is a good case for MUD when you lead from x x x against a suit contract. Against no-trumps the lead from a doubleton is after all rare, and from 6 4 3 we recommend the 6. In the middle of the hand MUD may be useful.

SIGNALS AND ECHOES

Some good players are lazy signallers, but all good signallers are effective defenders. This is an area where teamwork really pays and there is a notable difference between rubber bridge and tournament practice.

Signalling methods have evolved in a haphazard way and are surely open to improvement. The main problem is that players may want to say many things but for the most part have only one way of communicating: they can play high-low or not play high-low. (There are other possible ways of sending a message, as we point out later; but for the moment we refer to existing methods.)

As matters stand, players exchange messages in only one way and on only three subjects:

(1)   Strength in the suit played.
(2)   Length in the suit played.
(3)   Strength in a different suit. (That is, suit-preference.)

The key question in any signalling situation is, 'To which of those three does a high (or low) spot card relate?' The traditional approach has been to classify different situations in advance, but a more flexible method, based on a single principle, will work better. The thought in the mind of the player who emits the signal should not be *What message do I want to send?* but *What message will partner want to receive?*

This question is usually quite easy to answer. Here is a typical case where it will dispel the present uncertainty:

North
♠ J
♡ 10 7 6 3
♢ Q J 6
♣ A Q 10 8 3

East
♠ 7 4 2
♡ Q 8 2
♢ 9 8 5 3
♣ 7 6 2

♡ K led

South	West	North	East
—	1 ♡	Pass	Pass
2 ♠	Pass	3 ♣	Pass
4 ♠	All pass		

East's first problem is which card to play on the lead of ♡ K, partner having bid the suit. A rubber-bridge player, accustomed to signalling strength rather than length, would contribute the 8. A tournament player in East's situation would recognise that it was not so simple: the defenders have got to cash quickly, so partner will want to know about length. Even so, East might be uncertain which signal to give.

The correct play emerges clearly when the test mentioned above is applied. What does partner want to know? Obviously, *how many* hearts you hold. So you play the 2, denoting an odd number. At trick 2 West shifts to ♢ K. Now the average rubber-bridge player would drop a despondent 3, telling West nothing he did not know already. The 5, beginning a mild echo to show an even number, is clearly more informative.

Good signalling really is that simple. If you follow out our suggestions you will come up with new answers in quite a few familiar situations. We study the matter now under these headings:

(1) Signals at suit contracts.
(2) Signals at no-trumps.
(3) Further messages.

1. SIGNALS AT SUIT CONTRACTS

An echo with low cards either invites a continuation or indicates an even number of cards. When third hand holds a doubleton the two motives generally coincide, but it is standard practice to start an echo even when they do not.

North
Q 10 7 5 2

East

K led   6 4

West has bid the suit he is leading, so there is an obvious danger that a continuation may be ruffed. A suit-length signal is the message West will most want to receive, so East makes the normal play of the 6.

When three or more cards are held, the first meaning of an echo is to show encouragement. The second meaning—which prevails when it is evident that third hand can have no useful message to convey about strength—is suit length. We saw an example above. Here are two others:

North
(1)   Q 10 4

East

K led   J 9 5 2

As the location of the key cards is apparent to everyone, East's signal should be related to length. Partner will almost always be able to gauge that the 5 is from four, not two.

Here again it is obvious that East can only be signalling length:

North
(2)   A J 6 2

East

K led   8 7 3 or 8 7 4 3

Whether declarer plays the Ace or not, the only message West can want to receive will be related to suit length. With 8 6 3 East should play the 3, with 8 6 4 3 the 4.

Note that the usual card to indicate four is the second from the bottom. An eccentric play such as the Jack from

J 9 5 2, or even the 8 from 8 7 4 3, will then serve as a suit-preference signal.

In the examples above, the lie of the high cards has been clear as soon as the dummy has gone down, so a signal to show strength would be superfluous. But what of this next situation?

	North
(3)	A 9 3
	East
5 led	J 8 2

On the lead of the 5 the declarer goes up with the Ace in dummy. If West has led from a holding such as Q 10 x x he will know that East holds the Jack. Therefore it is correct to play the 8 only if a continuation is particularly desired: otherwise the 2 is more informative.

This is a similar position:

	North
(4)	A 8 4
	East
2 led	Q 10 9 5 3

On the lead of the 2 declarer goes up with the Ace. An unimaginative player might think it expedient to signal the Queen by dropping the 10, but it will already be perfectly clear to West that declarer does not hold that card. East should play the 3, indicating an odd number. That may help partner to judge whether or not the defence can take a trick in the suit.

As you see, there are no set rules for signalling, only a general principle: work out what partner knows already and aim to tell him something new. Here are some more plays which conform to that idea.

The unfinished echo

We have said that the first meaning of an echo is to express encouragement. When he would be happy with a continuation a player may begin an echo even when he holds nothing of worth in the suit led.

North
873

East
K led   1062

West has overcalled in the suit and is likely to hold five or more cards. If East does not want to suggest a switch he should play the 6 and on the next round the 10. If declarer follows to this trick West will know that East holds the missing card, as with 62 he would have echoed. The point of this type of play is not so much to 'master-mind' the situation by giving an unorthodox signal as to tell partner something he may not already know—that it is safe to continue.

Suit-preference on the second round

This is another type of signal that can be made when third hand holds only small cards:

10 63

KQJ82   974

A5

West leads the King, East plays the 4 and declarer wins with the Ace. Later in the hand West leads the Queen and East has the option of playing the 7 or the 9. As the card he plays can have no importance in relation to the suit being played, there is opportunity for a suit-preference signal. The 9 would be a request for the higher suit and the 7, while not expressly a request for the lower suit, would at least deny particular interest in the higher.

One of the present authors thought he saw the chance for an improvised signal when he held the East cards in a Masters Individual a few years ago.

```
              ♠ 8 5 4 3
              ♡ Q 9 8
              ◇ J 8 3
              ♣ A 7 2
♠ 10 7                      ♠ J 9
♡ K J 7 4                   ♡ A 6 5
◇ 2                         ◇ K 10 7 6 5 4
♣ K Q J 8 6 5               ♣ 9 3
              ♠ A K Q 6 2
              ♡ 10 3 2
♣ K led       ◇ A Q 9
              ♣ 10 4
```

South	West	North	East
—	Pass	Pass	Pass
1 ♠	2 ♣	2 ♠	All pass

Playing in Two Spades, declarer won the club opening and led ◇ J from dummy. East played low and the Jack held. On the next diamond lead East put up the King, intended as suit-preference for a heart shift. Apparently West saw nothing unusual in this sequence of play, for after ruffing the second diamond he continued clubs, missing the chance of another diamond ruff.

Signals from a long suit

The opening leader, as is well known, can often give a suit-preference signal at trick 1. Suppose he has overcalled in hearts and holds K J 9 7 4 3: a lead of the 7 would be normal fourth best, while the 9 or the 3 would contain suit-preference implications.

Now take a situation where the leader's partner holds a long suit. In this example the Ace is led and we will suppose that both players know a second round will not stand up.

```
              1 0 6 2
A 8 5                      K J 9 7 4 3
              Q
```

The principle to follow is that the extreme cards—in this instance the Jack and the 3—are suit-preference. The middle cards—the 9 and the 4—are normal encouragement or discouragement.

The trump echo

The echo to show three trumps is standard practice, but there has been a change of emphasis. The main purpose used to be to alert partner to the possibility of a ruff, but now it is normal to echo whenever the information about trump length is more likely to be helpful to partner than to declarer. The signal is particularly important when a defender sees that he may have a winning trump after two rounds.

(1)   K 9 6 3
          J   Q 10 8
                             A 7 5 4 2

Whether South leads small from dummy or the Ace from hand, East should echo. Otherwise, West may not know after two rounds have been drawn that his partner holds a third trump.

(2)   A 10 8 4
          Q   J 9 7
                             K 6 5 3 2

Here East should begin an echo whether declarer starts by playing low from dummy or the King from hand.

Of course, there are many occasions where the trump distribution is better known to the defenders than to the declarer, and naturally they will not want to assist him. It is particularly unwise to issue honest signals in the trump suit when declarer is in a 4-3 or 5-2 fit, for his entire strategic plan may depend on whether he judges the trumps to be 3-3 or 4-2.

A defender who holds four trumps can usually communicate this at once by dropping his lowest card on the first round. Further messages can then be conveyed on the second and third rounds. With a negligible holding such as 8 5 4 3, start with the 3, and echo with the 5 and 4, telling partner that you have no trump trick by right. With a holding capable of developing a natural trick, such as J 9 5 3, play upwards.

Finally, a player who leads trumps should indicate whether

he holds two or three. With 4 2 lead the 2; with 7 4 2 lead the 4 and play the 2 on the next round.

2. SIGNALS AT NO-TRUMPS

At no-trumps, as in a suit contract, the first meaning of a high card is encouragement; the second, when it is clear that the signal is not based on high cards, is suit length.

	North	
(1)	8 5 3 2	
		East
K led		J 6 4

	North	
(2)	Q 10 4	
		East
K led		9 6 3 2

On the lead of the King, East signals with a middle card in each case. He would do the same in a suit contract. There is a difference in the play from a doubleton. At a suit contract it is normal to echo, but that is not the present method at no-trumps, where a doubleton is no asset. The result is that at no-trumps the same low card is played from x x x and from x x.

We said earlier that signalling conventions had developed in a haphazard way, and this is the outstanding example. It is as important at no-trumps to be able to distinguish between three cards and two as it is at suit contracts, yet often the means does not exist. Consider these familiar situations:

	North	
(3)	A 7 4	
West		
K Q 10 8 5	2 played	

On the lead of the King (or Queen, if Roman leads are in use) dummy plays the 4 and East plays the 2. West does not know whether declarer holds J x or J x x.

(4)   *North*
                             Q J 3
          West
          K 10 8 5 2   4 played

West leads the 5 and dummy's Queen wins, East dropping the 4. Later, West gains the lead in another suit. If he knew his partner held three cards originally he would continue and find the blank Ace.

What we are coming to, as the reader will have gauged, is the proposal that the standard signal to show length at no-trumps should be the highest from *three* cards. (Note that this principle is already followed in the trump echo, where the important distinction is between three cards and other holdings.) With four cards echo with the third and fourth highest. No signalling method will clear up all situations without fail, but the play of a high card from three will resolve most problems including (3) and (4) above. Here are some other examples:

(5)   K 7 4
          Q J 9 6 2   8 5 3
                             A 10

West's lead of the Queen runs up to declarer's Ace. East's play of the 8 tells West that it will be safe to continue with the Jack later.

(6)   A 8
          Q J 10 5 3   6 2
                             K 9 7 4

West's Queen is headed by dummy's Ace and East plays the 2. West can tell at once that his partner has a doubleton at most.

(7)   Q 6
          A J 10 9 3   8 7 5 2
                             K 4

West leads the Jack and declarer puts in the Queen. The 5 appears from East and the 4 from South. West cannot be sure of the distribution as yet, but he can place his partner with two or four.

The same system can be followed with advantage when declarer is attempting to take tricks in dummy's suit.

(8)   K Q J 8 4
            9 6 3   A 10 5
                        7 2

A resourceful declarer will lead the 7, concealing the lowest card. At present, when a second honour is led from the table, East may be uncertain whether his partner's 3 was from 9 6 3 or the beginning of an echo from 3 2. In most situations of this kind the top card from three will be a clearer signal. West should play the 9 on the first round.

THREE FURTHER MESSAGES

We conclude with a few enticing novelties—signals that can be included in the general scheme without creating any confusion.

The six-shooter

Take the situation where a player leads from a long suit and subsequently discards from it. He has an opportunity now to tell partner his length in the suit, and we suggest that a high card should show exactly six cards. This is an example:

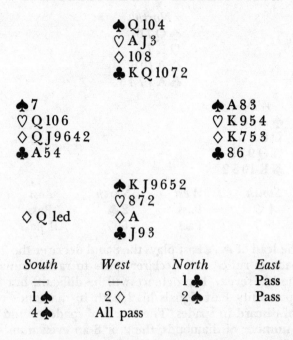

```
                    ♠ Q 10 4
                    ♡ A J 3
                    ◇ 10 8
                    ♣ K Q 10 7 2

  ♠ 7                                  ♠ A 8 3
  ♡ Q 10 6                             ♡ K 9 5 4
  ◇ Q J 9 6 4 2                        ◇ K 7 5 3
  ♣ A 5 4                              ♣ 8 6

                    ♠ K J 9 6 5 2
                    ♡ 8 7 2
  ◇ Q led           ◇ A
                    ♣ J 9 3
```

South	West	North	East
—	—	1♣	Pass
1♠	2◇	2♠	Pass
4♠	All pass		

South wins the diamond lead and plays trumps, East winning the second round. Now a likely defence for East is to lead a low diamond, trusting partner to win and lead a heart through dummy. On the second round of trumps, however, West discards a high diamond, the 9, to show precisely six. East can now see that the only chance is to attack hearts. The 'six-shooter', as we call this signal, will also be useful in a negative way when the player with the long suit (not necessarily the leader) discards a low card.

The periscope

When a player's exact holding in a long suit is already known to his partner, then clearly any message he sends should be designed to light up the situation elsewhere. We suggest that the first discard from such a suit should relate to the higher-ranking of the two other suits, an even card denoting an even number, an odd card an odd number. The following example is given from the angle of West, the player who receives the signal:

North
♠ Q 7 6
♡ K 7
♢ A 10 6
♣ A J 7 4 3

West
♠ A 10 4
♡ 8 3
♢ Q 9 7 5
♣ K 10 8 2

South	West	North	East
1 ♡	Pass	2 ♣	Pass
3 ♡	Pass	6 ♡	All pass

On the lead of ♣ A East plays the 8 and declarer the 9. The next spade is ruffed and declarer starts to rattle trumps, of which he has seven. The defence will be difficult, but at his first opportunity East signals his length in diamonds by his choice of discard in spades. The 3 or 5 of spades would show an odd number of diamonds, the 2 or 8 an even number. If East had no card of the required parity he would throw an unnecessarily high card of the other type. The discard will give West an immediate clue to declarer's most likely distribution and will help him to guard the right suit.

Both the periscope and the six-shooter can be used equally in a suit contract and at no-trumps. The periscope is the only example we give here of the use of odd or even cards to convey a message. This seems to be a strangely neglected stratagem.

The oddball

There are many occasions when one defender knows that his side is dead unless partner will make an inspired play. You know the sort of thing. You want partner to make an improbable switch, such as the Queen from Q x x through dummy's K x x x. You have set-up suit at no-trumps, if only he would attack it from a holding such as K x. You have a shortage where he will not expect it and you are praying for a ruff.

There is a simple way to cover all the possibilities. Any

uncharted signal conveys this message: 'There's something in the air.'

The first opportunity to make such a signal will usually occur when declarer cashes winners in a suit. Say this is the distribution:

$$AQJ5$$
$$1083 \qquad 9742$$
$$K6$$

The normal play for West is the 3, 8, 10. To play 3, 10, 8 would be a mild suit-preference indication, meaning perhaps no more than that he proposed to keep a guard in the higher of the likely suits. Any other sequence would be 'the oddball'.

For East, the normal play would be 4, 2, 7, 9. Any unusual pattern, such as 2, 9, 4, 7, would cause West to sit up. Another example of an oddball would be middle-high-low in the trump suit.

Once he has spotted the oddball it is up to partner to interpret it. The first meaning of an irregular signal in a suit played by declarer at no-trumps should be, 'I am better than you might expect in the suit originally led.' How often have you wanted to send that message in situations like the following!

(1)
$$74$$
$$A1083 \qquad Q9752$$
$$KJ$$

West's lead of the 3 is headed by the Queen and King. When in the lead again, West can hardly be expected to bang down the Ace unless East, meanwhile, has indicated his good holding by a 'surprise' signal.

(2)
$$853$$
$$97 \qquad AQJ64$$
$$K102$$

West leads a short suit, East puts in the Jack, and the King wins. East must aim to clarify the position, lest West stab in a different direction when next in.

(3)   Q 7 4
                          9 6 5 2   A J 10 3
                                       K 8

West leads the 2, dummy plays low, and East's 10 is headed
by the King. West knows little about the situation until his
partner gives the signal.

In the next example the message cannot mean anything in
respect of the suit led, so West must seek another
explanation :

                                    ♠ Q 6
                                    ♡ A 9 8 2
                                    ◇ J 9 7 3
                                    ♣ K 7 3

       ♠ J 10 5 3   ♠ 9 7 4 2
       ♡ J 10 7 6   ♡ Q 5 3
       ◇ A 2   ◇ K Q 10 5
       ♣ Q 10 2   ♣ 8 6

                                    ♠ A K 8
                                    ♡ K 4
          ♡ 6 led   ◇ 8 6 4
                                    ♣ A J 9 5 4

South	West	North	East
1♣	Pass	1◇	Pass
1NT	Pass	2NT	Pass
3NT	All pass		

West's lead of the 6 of hearts is covered by the 8, Queen
and King. South plays a club to the King and returns a club
to the Jack and Queen. On these two tricks East plays the 8
and 6. There would be no sense in an echo to show length, so
West looks for the hidden meaning. On this occasion the
message cannot relate to hearts, the suit led, for dummy still
has a double guard. The meaning must be, 'Don't make the
obvious switch to spades'. So, just in time, West lays down
the Ace of diamonds!

SUMMARY OF LEADS AND SIGNALS

This summary is limited to the new or comparatively new ideas that have been advanced.

Leads

Adopt Roman leads—the second highest from an honour sequence.

Usually play MUD leads (Middle, up, down) against a suit contract, but without a firm commitment.

Signals

In general, consider what signal partner will want to receive—a signal about strength or about length.

When signalling from a long suit on the opening lead, play middle cards to encourage or discourage, extreme cards to indicate suit-preference.

Normally echo with three trumps. With four trumps play the lowest first, then echo when the trumps held are of negligible rank.

At no-trumps play the highest card from three small as a length signal. With four cards echo with the third and fourth highest.

When discarding from a long suit which has already been played, throw a high card to denote precisely six.

When discarding from a long suit where your length is known, throw an even card to denote an even number of cards in the higher-ranking of the other two suits, an odd card to denote an odd number.

Make a 'surprise' signal when you want partner to take unexpected action; in particular, at no-trumps make an irregular play in declarer's suit to stress a good holding in the suit originally led.

13

MATCH PLAY

A team-of-four match is not, in a technical sense, so testing as pairs play. Competitive bidding is not so intense and overtricks are relatively unimportant. On the other hand, there is a keener sense of personal combat, a more direct test of nerve and morale. A much tighter game is necessary, for it may be difficult to get the points back after a fanciful bid or play. We say more about these aspects later, but first we look at the mathematical odds that govern bidding in team play.

THE ODDS IN AN UNCONTESTED AUCTION

Total-point scoring is now almost unknown and matches between two teams are decided by the International Match Point scale, known as IMP.

Difference in points	IMP	Difference in points	
			13
			14
20-40	1	750-890	15
50-80	2	900-1090	16
90-120	3	1100-1290	17
130-160	4	1300-1490	18
170-210	5	1500-1740	19
220-260	6	1750-1990	20
270-310	7	2000-2240	21
320-360	8	2250-2490	22
370-420	9	2500-2990	23
430-490	10	3000-3490	24
500-590	11	3500-3990	
600-740	12	4000 & upwards	

This scoring table is much closer to rubber bridge than the scoring in pairs. If you stay in a part score while opponents bid and make a non-vulnerable game it will cost you about 6 points; if you bid the game and go down one, opponents stopping in a part-score, it will cost you about 5. Thus it is right to bid a game which is slight odds against—as at rubber bridge.

Vulnerable, it is right to press, for now a missed game costs 10 points, while the gain is only 6 if you make a part score while opponents go one down.

The odds required for a small slam are the same as at rubber bridge. Not vulnerable, a winning slam gains 11 IMP, a losing one costs about the same. Vulnerable, the proportions are similar. So you want even money for any small slam contract.

Grand slams, however, are appreciably more attractive than at rubber bridge, where odds of at least 2 to 1 on are required. Not vulnerable, the gain is 11 IMP (as compared with a small slam), while the loss is 15 if the grand slam fails and opponents make Six. Vulnerable, the figures are 13 and 19. Thus when not vulnerable you are (mathematically) right to bid a grand slam when the odds are as good as 11 to 8 in your favour; vulnerable, you need about 6-4.

THE ODDS IN A CONTESTED AUCTION

At match play, sacrifices against vulnerable opponents are more rewarding than at any other kind of scoring. If you concede 500 to save a vulnerable game you gain a useful 3 or 4 IMP, and if you misjudge slightly and lose 700 the cost is only 1 or 2 points. You have a very wide latitude for sacrifices against slam contracts. Penalty doubles, on the other hand, are less attractive than at other forms of scoring. The foreshortening effect of the IMP scale reduces the profit from a sizeable penalty, and if only a one-trick set is expected the odds are against the doubler.

We turn now to the human side of tournament bridge.

THE PERSONAL FACTOR IN MATCH PLAY

This book has been mainly concerned with technique, but as every player knows, there is a lot more to the game than that. Much of the fascination of tournament bridge lies in the struggle of personalities, which at the higher levels counts for more than slight differences of skill. The reason why some players are just a bit more effective than others is that they deploy every resource of brain and character, not just their technical knowledge.

There are certain qualities which you will find in every serious player. First, he plays each hand for the maximum. Like a golfer who goes through the same routine on the eighteenth green whether he is in the money or down the field, he will devote the same sort of care to a part-score contract on the last board as to a slam on the first. It is not that he minds whether he finishes one place higher or lower: it is a matter of maintaining his own standards.

That sort of spirit leads to consistency, perhaps the most important single attribute of a tournament player. Anyone who plays up to his own standard, making only such mistakes as he is not capable of avoiding, is hard to beat at any game.

The next requirement is a proper respect for theoretical knowledge. Apart from the fact that some hands are difficult to set about if the necessary technique is lacking, the game is much less wearing for a player who, as they say, has been there before. You can learn from books and articles, and still more from constant practice in good company. In every circle the best players tend to be those who play the most, rubber as well as tournament bridge.

Determination, steadiness, and sound technique, then, are all necessary qualities. But that is not the end of it—there is the imponderable element of personality. Some players and partnerships convey an air of daunting superiority, some of such calm technical competence that it seems vain to hope for an error. Some give the appearance of seeing everything in a flash, others meditate so long you wonder how deep is the ocean of their minds. If you can develop an aura that creates a positive impression, you will have that much more going for you.

PREPARING FOR A MATCH

Nerves are not an important factor for most players—at least, they tend to be forgotten when the game gets under way. If you yourself take a little time to get going, the best preparation for a key match is a rubber or two. Then you will have your eye in from the start.

Different forms of contest call for a different outlook. Take first a straight team-of-four match of 48 boards. A good mental approach is to assume that you start with a lead of 50 match points. That allows an equal number for bad luck, for the total errors of your opponents will surely add up to 100 points (only 2 points a board for the whole team). Think back: can you remember ever losing a match against opponents of comparable ability when your squad played reasonably well? Luck makes a difference—but not that much difference.

For the first half, at any rate, the game is simply to avoid throwing points away. If at half-time you are down, you must be a bit more enterprising. But don't overdo it. Very few matches are won by pressing in the second half, but many a match is 'done in' twice over when a team which has had every chance to recover from a bad start throws points away through foolish extravagances.

Remember, above all, that you are part of a team. If your opponents get one or two good results, don't panic and make peculiar bids or plays. Your pair in the other room may be playing well too. If not, there's always next year!

Duplicate, and multiple team contests, must be approached in a different spirit. Unless you are very lucky you won't win a pairs event without displaying some initiative. It is true that an unbroken sequence of average-plus scores will win, but you must budget for an occasional bottom, caused through no fault of your own. Therefore you should go for a good board whenever you see the chance. In short, start a team game with the determination not to lose, a pairs with the determination to win.

RHYTHM IN BIDDING AND PLAY

Is it better to play quickly or slowly? Anyone who can play quickly and well has an advantage, but more important is to play at an even pace. Play at your own tempo and don't be put out of your stride by a declarer who tries the 'rap-rap' game.

Always take time out to assess the situation when the dummy goes down, whether you are attacking or defending. ('There is no need to apologise, 'I wasn't thinking about this trick.') Whether the hand is easy or difficult, whether you are playing for overtricks or for a desperate chance, maintain an impassive air and even rhythm.

Play the cards in a uniform manner, whether cashing a winner, taking a finesse, or making a deceptive play. (That precept is in fact easier to follow at tournament play, where the tricks are not gathered in, than at rubber bridge.) Most players, without realising it, give away information whenever they start thinking. Say that you have to make a blind lead against 3NT from:

♠ K J 6 3   ♡ Q 7 5   ◇ J 6 4 2   ♣ 10 9

Anything could be right; you know that from experience, and trancing won't bring you any closer to a logical answer. A player who hesitates over this lead is not cogitating—he is dithering. Meanwhile, an astute declarer will be thinking, 'He hasn't got a five-card suit, his four-card suits are unattractive, the suit he eventually leads may be a short suit'. So make your choice smoothly and promptly.

You can go to work on many lead and bidding problems before the ball is actually in your court. Even if you are not taking part in the auction, you can listen. The type of player who always wants a review of the bidding is seldom a fireball.

To keep ahead of the game is especially important when discarding on a declarer's long suit. Not only must the defender keep the right cards but he must study how to conceal his holding. Here the technique of the 'advance trance' is most important. A defender who sees he will be under the hammer later in the play must calculate how many discards he will have to make, what cards he must assume his partner to hold, and what suit he will be forced in the end to unguard. This thinking must be done before the pressure begins, so that nothing can be gleaned from later discards.

In a pairs event, especially, there is a great premium on

holding up high cards even when this leaves them unprotected. Suppose that you are East in this defensive situation:

K J 10 5
Q 8 6

Playing 3NT, declarer leads the 3, partner plays the 2, and the 10 is finessed. It will usually be good play to duck. The time may come later in the hand when declarer, having started with A x x, can make sure of his contract by cashing the Ace and King, but in the legitimate quest for overtricks he may finesse again, perhaps letting you win the last two tricks. Of course, it may happen in the meanwhile that partner will ruin the whole plan by discarding from three small. He'll know better next time!

MORALE

When things go wrong, different attitudes may be required with different partners. It is a mistake to make up one's mind to say nothing whatever happens. Some partners may prefer that, but not most. A player who has made a mistake wants most of all to justify himself. Give him this chance by discussing what has happened in a reasonable way. Aggressiveness towards partner is bad, but insincerity is worse.

Finally, there is the question of your relationship with the opponents. Suppose they make a mistake, letting you land a contract which could have been defeated. This is an occasion when good manners coincide with good tactics. Say nothing; if the opponents, determined not to find fault, remain silent, don't open a discussion, giving the player who has made a mistake a chance to explain. If they have an argument about a bid and are so ingenuous as to invite an opinion from your side, be deliberately vague and non-committal; let them wonder what you really think. Where the enemy's morale is concerned, your sentiments should be those of the poet who wrote:

> 'Thou shalt not kill; but needst not strive
> Officiously to keep alive.'